Know Your Men

Dag Heward-Mills

Unless otherwise stated, all Scripture quotations are taken from the King James Version of the Bible.

Originally published 2007 by Parchment House
ISBN: 978-9988-596-66-8
1st Printing 2007

This edition published 2008 by Lux Verbi.BM (Pty) Ltd.
PO Box 5, Wellington 7654, South Africa
Tel +27 21 864 8200
www.luxverbi-bm.com
Reg no 1953/000037/07
2nd Printing 2008

Copyright © 2007 Dag Heward-Mills

E mail Dag Heward-Mills :
bishop@daghewardmills.org
evangelist@daghewardmills.org

Find out more about Dag Heward-Mills at:
www.daghewardmills.org
www.lighthousechapel.org
www.healingjesuscrusade.org

Write to:
Dag Heward-Mills
P.O. Box 114
Korle-Bu
Accra
Ghana

ISBN 13: 978-0-7963-0963-1

All rights reserved under international copyright law. Written permission must be secured from the publisher to use or reproduce any part of this book, except for brie quotations in critical reviews or articles.

Dedication

To
Reverend Richard Aryee
Living far, yet so near
Thank you for your love for me and your faithfulness to me

Contents

1. Doubtful Men 7
2. Dangerous Sons 17
3. Bad Advisors 47
4. Painfully Disloyal People 69
5. The Scoffers 93
6. The Accusers 99
7. Forgetful Men. 107

Chapter 1

Doubtful Men

A doubtful person is someone whose loyalty comes into question from time to time. At times, the person may seem very loyal and at other times, disloyal.

Many people actually have this trait of being both loyal and disloyal. At times, they exhibit much loyalty and faithfulness and at other times, they are disloyal. It is important that you watch out for such people and note them carefully. They may be on your side or they may turn against you depending on the issue at hand.

I have such people around me and so does every leader. It is difficult to diagnose this mixture of loyalty and disloyalty. On more than one occasion, I have had people who named their children after me and hurt me at the same time. They did me the great honor of naming their sons after me.

Years ago, I read from Kenneth Hagin about how someone had named her child after him. I thought to myself, "what an honor" but I never imagined that someone would do me such an honor one day. To my amazement several people have named their children after me. I see it as a great and permanent honor done to me.

But how could someone bestow on me such honor and hurt my ministry at the same time? One pastor named his son after me and within a few months, he rebelled and took over the branch church he was pastoring. He renamed the church, led the congregation away and virtually stole our church. All this was done shortly after doing me a great honor. I have experienced this kind of mixed loyalty more than once.

You may live with such people for years and never realize how they undermine you constantly because they are also loyal to you.

I remember another member of my team who has supported the ministry for many years. I do not think I could find a more loyal person whom I expect to be with me in ministry till the very end. His support is like the support of Joab, long-standing and unflinching.

And yet in this same character, I have had a person who stirs up much dissension at meetings. On numerous occasions, his attitude stirred up discord amongst pastors, changed the course of happy fellowship times into sessions of debate, and heated discussions, which left us all with a sour taste when the meeting was over.

Over and over, he stirred up dispute in the name of being objective, frank and not being a "yes" man. He would often say that he was voicing the opinion of many who were simply not bold enough to bring out some of the issues. He did this with a good motive but the fruit of it was the disruption of pastoral meetings until I disliked having meetings with my own pastors. Because of the permanent and unflinching loyalty of this same pastor, I was always confused and could not place my finger on what I was dealing with.

It was years after these experiences that I realized that I was dealing with a mixture of both loyalty and disloyalty in the same person. I know that the seeds that were sown at these meetings were not good things because of the fruit they bore.

What was the fruit of these "objective" discussions? The fruit of these debates was to turn the heart of the father away from the sons. Without knowing it, I lost interest in my own pastors and turned away from them. I disliked having meetings with my own pastors and unconsciously avoided them.

The Holy Spirit does not flow in an atmosphere of disputes. Disputes and debates stir up differences of opinion that divide the team. Once the unity and oneness is broken, the environment for the anointing is gone. Constant, rancorous debate may be good for parliament but it is not good for building an anointed team.

We are to preserve the unity of the Spirit in an atmosphere of peace. "Endeavouring to keep the unity of the Spirit in the bond of peace" (Ephesians 4:3).

Joab: The Mixture of Loyalty and Disloyalty

Are there people in the Bible who are both loyal and disloyal? Yes. Joab is a good example of this mixture. His loyalty to David was long-standing. He supported David from the very beginning when David was not yet the king. Yet, Joab was a man who was both loyal and disloyal.

Joab is first mentioned when David was still a refugee in the wilderness being chased by Saul. Let us now look at the loyalty of Joab and how it coexisted with disloyalty.

Seven Demonstrations of Joab's Loyalty

1. Someone who supports you when you are not even in the ministry

Joab supported David when he was still a refugee. There are friends that God gives you from childhood. Some of these people are faithful as you progress in ministry. Such people are lifelong supporters. "Then answered David and said to Ahimelech the Hittite, and to Abishai the son of Zeruiah, brother to Joab, saying, Who will go down with me to Saul to the camp? And Abishai said, I will go down with thee" (1Samuel 26:6).

2. Someone who supports you at the beginning of your ministry, when everything is small and insignificant

Joab supported David when he was a king of only one tribe. Anyone who supports you when you are nothing is real. Never let him go. He is one of the best things that ever happened to you.

People who love you when you are already successful must go further to prove that they really love you and not the privileges of the rich and famous. "And Joab the son of Zeruiah, and the servants of David, went out, and met together by the pool of Gibeon: and they sat down, the one on the one side of the pool, and the other on the other side of the pool. And Abner said to Joab, Let the young men now arise, and play before us. And Joab said, Let them arise" (2 Samuel 2:13-14).

3. Someone who fights many battles and quarrels many quarrels for you

What a blessing it is to have someone who fights for you and takes some nasty blows on your behalf. Joab fought many wars on behalf of David. "And, Behold, the servants of David and Joab came from pursuing a troop, and brought in a great spoil with them..." (2 Samuel 3:22).

4. Someone who eliminates rebels and other disloyal elements from the team

Joab killed several people whose loyalties were questionable. He just could not stand people who were not totally committed to his king. He had an eye that saw these disloyal people whom people seemed to accommodate.

First of all he killed Abner who had supported Ishbosheth, the son of Saul for many years. "And when Abner was returned to Hebron, Joab took him aside in the gate to speak with him quietly, and smote him there under the fifth rib, that he died, for the blood of Asahel his brother" (2 Samuel 3:27).

Secondly, he killed Absalom, the son of David who overthrew his own father. "Then said Joab, I may not tarry thus with thee. And he took three darts in his hand, and thrust them through the heart of Absalom, while he was yet alive in the midst of the oak" (2 Samuel 18:14).

Thirdly, he killed Amasa who was appointed by Absalom as the commander of the armies that faught against King David. "But Amasa took no heed to the sword that was in Joab's hand: so he smote him therewith in the fifth rib, and shed out his bowels to the ground, and struck him not again; and he died" (2 Samuel 20:10).

5. Someone who constantly recognizes your position and refuses to take your honor

Joab called for David to come and receive the honor of victories he had won in war. He did not take that honor for himself. Most assistants would like to take some honor for themselves. They want everybody to know that it is really a team effort that is yielding results.

A God-given loyal assistant is happy as long as his leader gets the credit. "And, Behold, the servants of David and Joab came from pursuing a troop, and brought in a great spoil with them…" (2Samuel 3:22)

In spite of all these acts of loyalty, there are assistants who also have disloyal tendencies lurking within them. They will support you and they will fight you. It is an interesting combination that most leaders are never able to deal with because they simply don't understand that they are dealing with someone who is both loyal and disloyal.

6. Someone who stays with you to the very end; it is not easy to find people who will be with you all your life.

That is the kind of person Joab was; he was there until the end. "Now the days of David drew nigh that he should die; and … Joab" (1 Kings 2:1-5).

7. Someone who will obey virtually every command

Joab's intense loyalty to David is shown by the way he killed Uriah, one of his own men, upon David's instructions. All he needed was a note from David and he would act on it. Joab obeyed the instructions in David's letter. He needed no explanation in the note. David did not have to see Joab personally to explain how he had mistakenly impregnated Bathsheba. If David said to kill one of the commanders, then it would be done.

There are few people a leader can find, who have such unconditional and excessive loyalty. "And it came to pass in the morning, that David wrote a letter to Joab ... And he wrote in the letter, saying, SET YE URIAH IN THE FOREFRONT OF THE HOTTEST BATTLE, and retire ye from him, that he may be smitten, and die. And ... Joab ... assigned Uriah unto a place where he knew that valiant men were" (2Samuel 11:14-16).

Three Demonstrations of Joab's Disloyalty

1.   Someone who disobeys clear instructions when it suits him

Joab killed people he did not like even though it was against David's wishes. Abner had killed Joab's brother, Asahel and Joab therefore had a personal score to settle with Abner. Joab killed Abner in spite of King David's clear instruction on this matter. Joab also killed Absalom even though David had clearly asked that Absalom should not be killed.

These actions clearly demonstrate the disobedience and disloyalty that was lurking within Joab. David never forgot the disloyalty of Joab, and on his deathbed, he instructed Solomon to execute Joab for these acts.

Perhaps David did not execute Joab himself because Joab had also been very loyal to him and fought many battles for him. "Moreover thou knowest also what Joab the son of

Zeruiah did to me, and what he did to the two captains of the hosts of Israel, unto Abner the son of Ner, and unto Amasa the son of Jether, whom he slew, and shed the blood of war in peace, ...Do therefore according to thy wisdom, and let not his hoar head go down to the grave in peace" (1Kings 2:5-6).

2. Someone who fights people you have appointed

David appointed Amasa to be the commander of the army in place of Joab. "And king David sent to Zadok ...say ye to Amasa, Art thou not of my bone, and of my flesh? God do so to me, and more also, if thou be not captain of the host before me continually in the room of Joab" (2 Samuel 19:11-13). But Joab tricked Amasa and killed him when he was not expecting it. "But Amasa took no heed to the sword that was in Joab's hand: so he smote him therewith in the fifth rib, and shed out his bowels to the ground, and struck him not again; and he died" (2 Samuel 20:10).

One of the things you must look out for is how people relate with those you have appointed. When you have a large church, this is perhaps the most revealing sign of disloyalty. Because people always have to deal with you through your representatives, you get to learn about their real feelings towards you by observing how they relate with those you have appointed. Somebody who does not accept your wife does not accept you.

I always note people who are in constant dispute with my administrators, General Overseers, personal assistants and secretaries. To me, it is one of the clearest signs of disregard, disrespect and dislike for me personally.

It has made me understand how God feels when we criticize and reject the men he has called and anointed.

To criticize someone God has called and appointed is to say that God lacks intelligence and has foolishly appointed the wrong people. When people habitually fight and oppose those I have appointed, it sends a clear message to me!

3. Someone who does not support your wishes

David chose Solomon to be the king but Joab supported Adonijah's attempt to be the king in place of Solomon. "Then Adonijah the son of Haggith exalted himself, saying, I will be king: and he prepared him chariots and horsemen, and fifty men to run before him. And he conferred with Joab the son of Zeruiah, and with Abiathar the priest: and they following Adonijah helped him" (1Kings 1: 5,7).

If you give somebody a name and people refuse to address the person by his new name, it is a demonstration of the people's rejection of your wishes, goodwill and authority.

It is surely a sign that reveals the heart of people. Also, if you give somebody a name and the person does not insist on being called by the new name, it reveals the extent to which your wishes and desires are accepted and supported by the person himself.

Dear leader, people will not tell you what is in their hearts because they cannot. Sometimes they do not even know what is in their own hearts. Watch out for people who do not support your wishes, desires and authority. Opposition exposes the hearts of people!

Chapter 2

Dangerous Sons

There are some people who come out of your spiritual loins and are in reality your sons. Even though they are your sons, they can cause you great pain. As a leader, you must not be surprised if the people you bring up and train turn on you like wild tigers.

There are sons who carry the spirit of Absalom and such people are truly dangerous sons. *I call them dangerous because they are a part of you and yet they fight you.* They claim your heritage! They even look like you but the spirit of Absalom upon them changes everything.

How can you identify a son who will rise up against you to kill you? As usual, the Bible is the best guide for everything.

Twelve Signs of Dangerous Sons

1. *A dangerous son is full of unforgiveness and bitterness.*

> And Absalom spake unto his brother Amnon neither good nor bad: for ABSALOM HATED AMNON, because he had forced his sister Tamar.
>
> 2 Samuel 13:22

> And Jonadab, the son of Shimeah David's brother, answered and said, Let not my lord suppose that they have slain all the young men the king's sons; for Amnon only is dead: for by the appointment of Absalom THIS HATH BEEN DETERMINED FROM THE DAY THAT HE FORCED HIS SISTER TAMAR.
>
> 2 Samuel 13:32

Absalom was someone who did not forgive his brother for raping Tamar. He nursed the hatred in his heart for two years. He planned his revenge and eventually carried it out. This world is a place of much offence. Many things will offend you in the church. Harboring bitterness is the last thing that a minister should do.

I believe that the greatest temptation for a minister is the temptation to be unforgiving. This one sin will cut you away from God's love. In the Old Testament, there were some basic requirements for being a priest. A priest was not supposed to have unhealed wounds and sores. Unhealed wounds become infected and pollute the whole body.

A priest or a pastor was not allowed to carry around unhealed wounds. "No man with a crippled foot or hand or who is hunchbacked or dwarfed, or who has any eye defect, or who has *festering or running sores* or damaged testicles. No descendant of Aaron the priest who has any defect is to come near to present the offerings made to the LORD by fire. He has a defect; he must not come near to offer the food of his God. He may eat the most holy food of his God, as well as the holy food; yet because of his defect, *he must not go near the curtain or approach the altar*, and so desecrate my sanctuary. I am the LORD, who makes them holy" (Leviticus 21:18-23 NASU).

A true minister working in the vineyard will be wounded over and over. Jesus was wounded many times but he forgave. That is the example we must follow.

There are two common wounds experienced by pastors: the wounds inflicted by ungrateful and disloyal people. It is unbelievable how people forget the extent to which you have been a blessing to them. They turn on you. Many ministers cannot handle the ingratitude and disloyalty of people. The inability to handle ingratitude often becomes the turning point of their lives and ministries.

In the last interview of his life, Derek Prince was asked whether he had any regrets. Amazingly, he said that he regretted not forgiving the people who had hurt him as quickly as he should have.

To have become a minister is to have received extra mercy from God. This mercy is over and above the grace that is shown the average person. "It is God himself, in his mercy, who has given us this wonderful work [of telling his Good News to others], and so we never give up" (2 Corinthians 4:1, Living Bible). We are therefore expected to show mercy and forgiveness to those who offend us.

One day, I went for a walk with a pastor who had been betrayed by his assistant. As he spoke about this fellow, I noticed that he was virtually trembling. He could not believe what this disloyal associate had done to him. He had repaid all the goodness he had shown him with a slap in the face. I could virtually see the running sores and the open wounds on my brother. I felt sympathy for him because he was genuinely hurt. But I also worried for him because I knew it could be the end of his ministry. You see, Absalom's unforgiveness was the beginning of his journey to desolation. Perhaps, Absalom would have been the King after David. But Amnon's wound turned Absalom into something else.

Pastors are turned into bitter personalities by wounds that are inflicted on them from outside. Your reaction to something can kill you.

Asthma is a disease that reminds me of unforgiveness. Asthma is simply an overreaction to substances that irritate the lungs. In an attempt to keep out further irritants, the airways constrict and breathing becomes difficult. Death happens when this reaction goes too far. Absalom overreacted to his brother's crime. As Absalom persisted on the road of unforgiveness, bitterness and revenge, he destroyed his life and ministry.

Somehow, God expects us to be even more forgiving. Perhaps the highest form of offence comes from spouses. Because marriage involves a physical and natural union, ministers are prone to multiple carnal wounds. Every minister must be resolute and unflinching in his or her resolve to be permanently married.

Never change your mind about your spouse. Do not allow your wounds and hurts to lead you into deception. All other options you may have on your mind will hurt you just as much as this marriage has. You do not have an option. Stay with what God has given you to the very end.

John Wesley was a good example of this. He had a difficult marriage but he stayed married to the same woman to the end of his life. Even though it was impossible to live with his wife, he remained married to her. He was separated from her but never divorced. Marriage is for life. Good or bad, God expects you to forgive and walk in love. Watch out for people who do not forgive and forget.

2. *Dangerous sons attack their brothers.*

Now Absalom had commanded his servants, saying, Mark ye now when Amnon's heart is merry with wine, and when I say unto you, Smite Amnon; then kill him, fear not: have not I commanded you? be courageous and be valiant.

2 Samuel 13:28

Dangerous sons exhibit features, which are worrying to the experienced eye. Attacking and killing your own brother is a very bad sign and a cause for concern. You must recognize the danger signs of ministers who attack other colleagues.

Many pastors do not realize that most of their discussions center on others and not on the Word of God. Constant analysis, criticism and mockery of fellow ministers are most common in the conversation of some pastors.

Many times, it is not even possible to share Scripture and revelations with one another. The discussion of jealous pastors seems to center on criticizing what someone else is doing. I have noticed myself drawing away from the company of such ministers.

3. Dangerous sons are not changed by years of hardship and difficulty

So Absalom dwelt two full years in Jerusalem, and saw not the king's face.

2 Samuel 14:28

Absalom suffered the hardship of living in exile for two years. One would have thought that he would undergo a change of heart. Watch out for pastors you have had to discipline and correct. The fact that they have been through punishment does not mean that they have repented. The spirit of unforgiveness and rebellion is simmering within.

I remember an employee whom we disciplined. He wrote an apology letter in which he said, "I was wrong and I apologize for what I did." After writing his letter, he was suspended from his work for some months. Somehow, after months of suspension, this dangerous son of mine rose up in rebellion against me. He attacked me and the church to which he had belonged.

At one point, he sent a message to me saying, "I will drive you out of this city." Perhaps, his intention was to spread enough bad stories about me until I was too embarrassed to stay in town.

Do these threats not sound familiar to you? Did Absalom not attempt to drive David out of Jerusalem? Actually, Absalom succeeded in driving David out of Jerusalem for some days.

The point is this: the spirit of Absalom is not corrected through punishment and even years of hard discipline. Do not be deceived into thinking that Absalom has changed just because he has been through a period of discipline, hardships or even poverty.

This explains why some people never apologize no matter what they go through. They may suffer so much but will not humble themselves and repent. Such people are simply Absalom reborn! Two years of exile and difficulty did not change the heart of Absalom. He became hardened and even more dangerous! A true "Absalom" is not humbled by his difficult experiences nor do they change him in any way!

4. Dangerous sons feel that they cannot be dismissed.

And Absalom answered Joab, Behold, I sent unto thee, saying, Come hither, that I may send thee to the king, to say, Wherefore am I come from Geshur? it had been good for me to have been there still: now therefore let me see the king's face; and if there be any iniquity in me, LET HIM KILL ME.

2 Samuel 14:32

Whenever a person feels indispensable he is a dangerous person to have around. Some people feel that they are untouchable and can never be dispensed with.

Absalom was someone who felt that he could not be sacked. He felt that he could not be transferred away.

We read about how Absalom told Joab that if King David found something wrong with him he should simply execute him.

Absalom felt that his father could not execute him. Absalom was sure that David could not punish or deal with him in a certain way.

These words of Absalom reveal the mindset of a dangerous person. "My father cannot sack me", "My father cannot discipline me", "My father cannot deal with me." In other words, I am untouchable and I know it!

Anyone who feels he is untouchable has developed the wrong attitude.

One day, I stood chatting with the most senior associate of a very large church. This man was seething because he had been transferred to another city.

The senior pastor had recognized the rebellion that was building up and had moved him quickly out of the church.

But this fellow had thought that he was untouchable. He had also thought that it was an insult to be moved away from the church headquarters.

We continued talking about his new position in a branch church.

He said, "I am a senior associate and I have worked here for many years. The concept of being transferred should not be applied to someone of my rank. I am above such things as being transferred."

He continued, "Even the *word* 'transfer' should never have been applied to me....."

This fellow had thought that he was untouchable. He thought he was secure in his position forever. Unfortunately, as soon as you begin to think of yourself as indispensable, you are becoming proud and deceived. Just like Absalom, your delusions will lead to your destruction. Pride always comes before a fall.

Sometimes, people sense that they are special and loved and they take advantage of this special place that they have.

That is also a mistake. There is always a Joab that will do the job that the father doesn't want to do.

There are circumstances that will eliminate a deluded and proud child from every good position he has. Try your luck and discover for yourself that no one is indispensable.

Dismiss Me if You Can

One time, a special son of mine behaved himself disrespectfully against the authority that was over him. There were several acts of insubordination. I tried to call him to reason with him but this person would not even answer the telephone.

He would hear my voice on his answer machine and realize that I was desperately trying to get in touch with him. But he would not bother to answer.

Over a period of several weeks, we all tried to get in touch with him and to talk with him. He rudely ignored us until one day, his supervisor managed to get him on the phone. A short conversation ensued and I always remember a chilling message that this young man sent to all of us.

The overseer asked him, "Do you understand what you are doing? Do you know how badly you are behaving? Do you know how serious the situation is? Do you understand the implications of what you are doing?"

He answered, "I do. I know what I am doing. I know the implications of everything."

His overseer said to him, "Then why are you doing what you are doing?"

He was insolently silent. Then he said, "Maybe you should sack me."

His overseer stuttered, "Did I hear you right? What did you say?"

He continued, "Any good organization would dismiss someone like me. It's up to you to dismiss me."

The conversation ended and the supervisor put down the phone in disbelief.

When the overseer told me about his conversation with this son of mine, I understood what was happening. You see this fellow felt that I could not sack him. He knew that he was special and he was pushing things to the limit. It is an "Absalom son" who knows that his father cannot kill him even when he deserves to die.

It was true that I could not easily dismiss him. Even after I received the invitation to sack this fellow, I decided to make one more manoeuver to avoid dismissing him.

I called his wife and told her to advise her husband to resign decently to prevent me from having to dismiss him. As a father, I was making a move to prevent a son from destroying himself completely! Absalom knew how much his father, David, loved him and he took advantage of it and said, "let him kill me if he can."

Even when Joab executed Absalom, David lamented sorely over him. "And the king was much moved, and went up to the chamber over the gate, and wept: and as he went, thus he said, O my son Absalom, my son, my son Absalom! would God I had died for thee, O Absalom, my son, my son! And it was told Joab, Behold, the king weepeth and mourneth for Absalom. And the victory that day was turned into mourning unto all the people: for the people heard say that day how the king was grieved for his son" (2 Samuel 18:33-19:2).

Untouchable Wives

Wives who feel they cannot be divorced equally fall into this category. Some wives become mean and rebellious as they misuse the power of the marriage covenant, which opposes divorce. They feel they cannot be dismissed, divorced or replaced! They sense their husbands' commitment to the Word of God and exploit their untouchable status to the maximum. They hide behind the curtain and manifest some of the ugliest behavior possible on their powerless husbands.

A married minister is like a toothless bulldog that can bark but cannot bite. He can warn, rant and rave, but he cannot dismiss! And the wives know it! Several ministers suffer silently at the hands of insane and wicked women who take full advantage of the "you can't divorce" clause. For-For-Forgive!*

5. *Dangerous sons think they can replace their fathers.*

> ... **Absalom said moreover, Oh that I were made judge in the land, that every man which hath any suit or cause might come unto me, and I would do him justice!**
>
> **2 Samuel 15:3-4**

"Absalom" has a desire to take over and replace his father.

Absalom thought himself to be as good as his father David. This is the spirit of Absalom. "I can and will replace my father now." This is different from a son who wishes to emulate his father in the spirit of humility. This is a "takeover" and "replacement" spirit.

---

*The expressions *"Mercy, Forgive"* etc are the author's coloquial expressions.

You Can Feel It

A bishop friend of mine could feel the spirit of Absalom all around him. He sensed these dangerous sons with takeover spirits hovering all around him in the ministry. These were hawks who felt their spiritual father was not relevant anymore.

He blurted out, "Some people are trying to retire me, but I cannot be retired!" He could sense that some people wanted him to leave the scene.

He continued, "What they don't know is that when I am gone, the 'thing' that was fighting me will begin to fight them"

Three Signs of the Replacement Spirit

Whenever such people start churches, they are unable to hide their desire to quickly become what their father is. An "Absalom" cannot hide the desire he has had for many years; the desire to take over and to replace his father.

Absalom said moreover, Oh that I were made judge in the land' (2 Samuel 15:3-4).

This cry of the first Absalom is the same cry of all the present day "Absaloms".

It is the unspoken wish of these dangerous sons!

It is interesting to watch these dangerous people operate. Their actions only reveal the bloodline from which they come. New and rebellious ministries founded by 'Absaloms' have certain features.

I want to show you three common features that I have noticed of churches and ministries that are started by dangerous sons with an Absalom spirit.

a. They love to locate their new church near the church that they broke away from.

These churches are often in the same area as their original church.

I remember when a church I used to attend had a very popular associate pastor breaking away. This man published leaflets with damaging information against our senior pastor. One Sunday morning he distributed these leaflets as we all came to church. However, an army of ushers eventually rose up and threw him out of the front door.

This fellow was bewildered and stood outside the church building amazed that people could be loyal to someone he thought was unqualified. He felt he had enough damaging information to make the entire flock follow him. Instead he had been thrown out by loyal ushers.

Amazingly, he went a hundred meters down the same road and rented a hall thinking that the whole church would follow him there. Within a few months, his new church collapsed. "Absaloms" are sometimes very predictable. God does not bless the work of Absalom.

b. Another characteristic of these dangerous sons is that they use names similar to ones which their fathers use.

For instance, if the father's church was called "Losers International", Absalom's church is usually called 'Defeat International'. On the other hand, if the father's church is called, "Heaven Chapel International," the Absalom's church is usually called something like "Paradise Chapel International". Even within the church, they usually give similar names to things. For instance if the father's church choir was called "the Roses", Absalom's church choir would be called "the Lilies". If cell groups were called 'home fellowships', Absalom's cell groups would also be called "house fellowships" etc. The reason for these similarities is that they are actually sons and a son has similar characteristics to his father. As I said, these "Absaloms" cannot hide their identity of being associated with their father.

In some cases, an "Absalom" would even keep the name of his father's ministry and fight over the name with him. I have seen three amazing examples of this; where a breakaway church insists on using the name of the original ministry, which it broke away from as its name. Amazing, isn't it?

   c. Dangerous sons practise things similar to what their fathers practise.

Because Absalom learnt all that he knows from his father, he usually has similar practices in his church. For instance if the father's church had a midweek service on Thursday, Absalom would have his midweek service on Thursday as well. If his father's church had buses picking up members, Absalom usually does the same.

These are just a few similarities that prove that Absalom is truly a son, but a dangerous son indeed!

6.   *Dangerous sons criticize their fathers.*

> **And Absalom said unto him, See, thy matters are good and right; but there is no man deputed of the king to hear thee. Absalom said moreover, Oh that I were made judge in the land, that every man which hath any suit or cause might come unto me, and I would do him justice!**
>
> **2 Samuel 15:3-4**

Absalom criticized his father's way of governing the country. Criticism is born of an evil spirit. There is simply nothing that justifies criticism. All of Scripture condemns this practice.

The Hog Vision

I once had a vision in which I found myself walking down a long lonely path in the midst of some mountains. Visibility was good and I could see for miles all around me. In the vision, I was chatting and walking with two other pastors.

At a point, I made a comment about a great man of God. My remark was not one of praise neither was it neutral: it was criticizing this man for something he had done.

As soon as the words came out of my mouth, I noticed a creature that I can best describe as a hog begin to walk in my direction. It was miles away and somewhere behind us but I noticed that it began to make its way towards me as soon as I made the remark. The creature seemed to have heard my critical remark. Somehow, the complaint was the signal for it to start moving towards me.

Initially, I thought the movement of that animal had nothing to do with me, but I felt uneasy and kept turning to see where it was.

To my dismay, it kept coming towards me. I realized that I was in danger and I turned round with my friends to face the creature as it walked rapidly and determinedly toward us. Finally, the creature caught up with us. To my surprise, the hog ignored my friends and leapt towards me, heading straight for my chest. I screamed as it entered my chest and then I woke up.

The Lord said to me, "Any time you criticize my servants, you attract evil spirits to your life." These evil spirits bring sickness, disease and other plagues into your life. I realized that it was a very dangerous thing to speak against any of God's servants.

I was truly terrified by that vision.

Any spiritual person will be hesitant to speak against God's anointed, no matter the reason. Miriam felt she had a good reason to speak against Moses. When she criticized him she was struck with leprosy and God asked her, "...wherefore then were ye not afraid to speak against my servant Moses?" (Numbers 12:8).

The Joshua Generation

The people that followed Moses never entered the Promised Land. They could not enter the Promised Land because of one thing: the spirit of complaining, murmuring, doubting and criticism.

So we see that they could not enter in because of unbelief.

Hebrews 3:19

How was this unbelief manifested? Unbelief is demonstrated by murmuring and complaining. The Israelites complained about everything. In the end, they did not enter the Promised Land. The Moses generation did not enter The Promised Land but the Joshua generation did.

The Joshua generation are the generation who put away complaining and grumbling.

The Promised Land will be inherited by the generation that stops murmuring. If you can stop all forms of murmuring and grumbling in your church, you will see God's promise for your ministry.

The Joshua generation knew all about the devastating effects of murmuring. The followers of Joshua promised to eliminate anyone who manifested even the faintest signs of grumbling. "And they answered Joshua, saying, All that thou commandest us we will do, and whithersoever thou sendest us, we will go. According as we hearkened unto Moses in all things, so will we hearken unto thee: only the LORD thy God be with thee, as he was with Moses. *Whosoever he be that doth rebel* against thy commandment, and will not hearken unto thy words in all that thou commandest him, *he shall be put to death*: only be strong and of a good courage" (Joshua 1:16-18).

Ham, the Dangerous Son

A son who grows up in your house and benefits from all that you have but still does not believe in you is a dangerous son. Such dangerous sons forget that they would not exist if their father had not been there. Such people forget that they would not be in the ministry if someone had not made it possible for them.

Ham found out that his father was drunk and decided to tell others about it. He scoffed at his own father! What Ham forgot was that if Noah had not built an ark, he would not even exist! If Ham had not been alive, how would he have been able to criticize his father Noah? That is why the curse of Ham is so severe. Do not criticize your father even if he is drunk. Pray for yourself that you will never have the same drinking problem.

The Cult Document

Once, I had some sons whom I raised and trained in the ministry. When I met them, they were ordinary Christians and very far from becoming ministers. I trained them and appointed them as pastors, set them in churches, encouraged them and protected them from things that destroy young ministers. There were times they made obvious mistakes that could have turned their congregations against them but I covered them and did not allow people to rebel against them.

On one occasion, when someone heard that I had been able to make a pastor out of one of them he exclaimed, "You are doing wonders!"

On another occasion, I defended this young pastor so much that I was accused of having ulterior motives. Sometimes, young ministers exhibit indefensible and unacceptable behavior. However, as a father, it is my duty to protect my sons until they are able to stand on their own two feet. Eventually, these fellows departed from my ministry and no longer belonged to our church. Relating with them became an unpleasant experience for me because I realized that I was dealing with dangerous sons.

These were sons, but like Absalom, became an unpleasant experience to their father. I longed for them and thought about them often. I wished to have an input in their lives. However, it was not to be so.

My greatest shock came when I received a document from them which was a teaching about cults. In this document, the characteristics of cults were outlined. How to identify cults, and stay away from them!

Unfortunately, these two sons of mine had discovered through this teaching that Lighthouse Chapel, the church which had raised them, had some characteristics of a cult. They had shared these "truths" amongst themselves and were now sending me a copy to learn from it. I received my copy of the cult document. They wanted me to identify for myself the characteristics of my ministry that made what I was doing cultlike.

Of course, I do not believe that I am the pastor of a cult. I pray for grace and mercy to be delivered from such a thing. However, I consider it a privilege to be derided for Christ.

These young men had forgotten, that the church in which they now saw the features of a cult, had ordained them into the ministry.

Is it not amazing that someone I raised would even think of me and my ministry in the light of a cult! I don't even know of outsiders who can say such things. But such is life. Sons and daughters should be careful when making comments about someone who has been their father!

When Jesus cast out devils, someone made a comment about his using the spirit of Beelzebub. Jesus issued the most solemn warning ever: "Wherefore I say unto you, All manner of sin and blasphemy shall be forgiven unto men: but the blasphemy against the Holy Ghost shall not be forgiven unto men. And whosoever speaketh a word against the Son of man, it shall be forgiven him: but whosoever speaketh against the Holy Ghost, it shall not be forgiven him, neither in this world, neither in the world to come" (Matthew 12:31-32).

7. *Dangerous sons influence others against their fathers.*

And with Absalom went two hundred men out of Jerusalem, that were called; and they went in their simplicity, and they knew not any thing.

2 Samuel 15:11

False leaders thrive on the ignorance of their followers. Some people utterly dislike my book "Loyalty and Disloyalty". The reason they do not like it is that it exposes the disloyalty in them.

Books on loyalty educate ordinary people in the church about the consequences of disloyalty. After such teachings, the ordinary church member easily identifies disloyal leaders. A grumbling, rebellious leader will stick out like a sore thumb and will not flourish where loyalty and disloyalty have been taught.

Once I was invited to preach at a church. There were several pastors who sat on the front row of that church. I preached about loyalty and disloyalty. They all smiled with me after the service and gave neutral and pleasant comments about the sermon.

They said things like: "I was blessed", "good preaching"' etc. Unfortunately, some of them actually hated the message. Later, one of them made a remark.

He said, "That book 'Loyalty and Disloyalty' is rubbish."

One of the pastors asked, "Does he not have anything else to preach about?"

Yet another said, "Is it only loyalty and disloyalty that he knows about?"

Not surprisingly, those who disliked the message were the disloyal pastors on the board. Within a few years, those disloyal pastors had left that church.

It is a clever strategy to discredit a helpful book to your ignorant followers so that they will never find out what is in it. An Absalom thrives on the ignorance and naivety of the people. Watch out for people who campaign against their fathers, trying to make you turn against your own father.

8. *A dangerous son steals the heart of the people from his father.*

And on this manner did Absalom to all Israel that came to the king for judgment: so ABSALOM STOLE THE HEARTS of the men of Israel.

2 Samuel 15:6

And there came a messenger to David, saying, THE HEARTS OF THE MEN OF ISRAEL ARE AFTER ABSALOM.

2 Samuel 15:13

Absalom needed to gain a following and he knew what to do. He had to win the hearts of the people. Unfortunately, Absalom had no right to the hearts of the people. That is why the Bible uses the phrase "he *stole* the hearts" of the people. Dangerous sons want what does not belong to them. The most valuable thing a leader possesses is the heart of his followers. If their hearts are with you, then you are in control.

Leadership is all about winning the hearts of those you lead. David was a leader and he built the nation of Israel virtually from scratch. When he realized that the hearts of the people were with Absalom, he knew that he had to flee.

"Absaloms" are usually handsome or gifted individuals. Unfortunately, it is gifted, anointed and successful ministers who are tempted to become "Absaloms". Absalom had long, flowing hair and must have been attractive. Every senior pastor must watch the "gifted" ones closely. It is a real temptation to become a dangerous son when you are gifted.

Mysteriously, the very gift that God gives can become a snare to you. As someone said, "Can you stand to be blessed?" Can you carry an anointing? Can you carry an anointing for long? Can you be gifted without become disloyal? Can you be a blessed son without becoming an Absalom? Can you be rich without becoming proud?

Can you have access to the people without stealing their hearts? Can anyone leave you in charge of his church without your taking over? Can someone found a church and leave it in your care for a year without your stealing the hearts of the people?

Do not let your gift become your snare. Eventually Absalom was captured and killed because of his long, flowing hair. The blessing that God gave you will become what destroys you. How common this is. "And Absalom met the servants of David. And Absalom rode upon a mule, and the mule went under the thick boughs of a great oak, and his head caught hold of the oak, and he was taken up between the heaven and the earth; and the mule that was under him went away" (2 Samuel 18:9).

9. *A dangerous son wants the pleasures and privileges of his father.*

So they spread Absalom a tent upon the top of the house; and Absalom went in unto his father's concubines in the sight of all Israel

2 Samuel 16:22

The privileges of a father are special. It is important to respect the privilege that God has given to fathers. A son who desires the privileges of his father is truly an Absalom. Many ministers claim that God led them to begin their ministries. Actually, some of these men are "Absaloms" who want to enjoy the privileges of their father.

They are not content with what they have and see no reason why they should slave away and let someone else get all the big benefits.

If God has called you to start your own ministry, please make sure that you are not just another Absalom desiring the pleasure and privileges of senior pastors. The spirit of Gehazi and the spirit of Absalom merge at this point.

Gehazi desired more privileges and Absalom took ten of his fathers concubines. "Absaloms" want more cars, houses and money. They want to be great and they want it quickly. It is the fight for privileges that is often called the fight for "truth". In the name of fighting for the truth or fighting for God's will to be done, people are actually fighting for more privileges and pleasure spots. Forgive!

10. Dangerous sons have destructive tendencies.

> **Therefore Absalom sent for Joab, to have sent him to the king; but he would not come to him: and when he sent again the second time, he would not come. Therefore he said unto his servants, SEE, JOAB'S FIELD is near mine, and he hath barley there; go and SET IT ON FIRE. And Absalom's servants set the field on fire.**
>
> 2 Samuel 14:29-30

Absalom burnt down Joab's farm in order to get his attention. He would stop at nothing in order to have his way. Watch out for people who would stop at nothing to have their way.

They spend money recklessly and drive over people to have their way. You can see the ruthlessness in Absalom by this act of burning Joab's farm. A ruthless person is a dangerous person. In their quest for power, they will do anything. They do not mind burning down the entire ministry or the reputation of their fathers in order to get their way.

11. Dangerous sons are men of conspiracies, secret meetings and side discussions.

> **And Absalom sent for Ahithophel the Gilonite, David's counsellor, from his city, even from Giloh, while he offered sacrifices. AND THE CONSPIRACY WAS STRONG; for the people increased continually with Absalom.**
>
> 2 Samuel 15:12

Absalom had several secret meetings with Ahithophel and other dissenters. These quiet meetings were necessary to develop a strong conspiracy.

There are people who love to whisper among themselves even in your presence. Whatever they say never seems to concern you! It is time to discern and to detect conspiracies among so-called loyal followers.

The success of any mission depends on the absolute loyalty of those with you. Fight for loyalty.

Keep your eyes open and notice people who have meetings after the official meeting, discussions on the side and private jokes, which no one else understands. These are all signs that there is hidden information which is being kept from you.

12. *Dangerous sons lack the ability to induce loyalty in their followers.*

Dangerous sons are doomed to failure in ministry because they have been castrated of the power to induce loyalty. The testicles of loyalty have been removed and therefore there are no more seeds that generate loyal followers.

After leading armies of people to kill your own father, how will you be established as a father?

The very foundation of loyalty and commitment is destroyed. The people you led have watched you destroy your own father. *They have learnt by example about how to overthrow established and God-ordained leaders.*

Removing Foundations

I remember visiting a pastor friend of mine who had just taken over a branch church of a certain denomination. He had painted over the original name of the church and renamed it.

He, together with the associates had conspired to rebel against the denominational headquarters and seize the entire church, including its assets, properties and members.

I challenged my friend, "How could you do something like this?"

Standing in the auditorium with him, I pointed out, "That is not your pulpit, and these are not your chairs."

I continued, "It is wrong to take over a church in this way."

But he was adamant, arguing that it was the will of God.

He explained, "Our General Overseer is backslidden and does not read the Bible any more. He just reads strange books like 'Attila the Hun'".

"What is Attila the Hun?", I asked.

He answered, "I don't even know what 'Attila the Hun' is about because I refuse to read such things instead of the Bible"

Then he said, "Come, let me show you something."

He took me outside and there was a brand new, gleaming, black, German executive car. He said, "A man who heard of my takeover, bought this brand new car and sent it to me as a gift to encourage me. He did this to say 'thank you' to me for a good work done".

As we stood by this beautiful car, the pastor turned and looked into my face and said, "Can this be the devil? Is this not God at work? Would the devil give me such a beautiful and expensive car?"

To him, this surprise gift of a brand new car was a confirmation that he had done the right thing.

Then I asked, "How are you going to lead this new church?"

He said, "I am the pastor, but the others around me are going to have a share of the leadership. I don't want to run a one-man show as my former General Overseer did."

"I will be a different kind of leader," he continued.

As we parted company, I knew that this brother had removed the foundations for stability, leadership and loyalty. A few months later, his new associate pastors asked him to leave them. They leveled various accusations against him and showed him the door. He had no control over his associates because there was no foundation to that church. He was now powerless to control the raging storms of rebellion that he had unleashed.

Can you believe that within a few years, the other pastors who assisted him threw him out of the church? You cannot build on foundations that you have destroyed.

Doomed to Reap a Harvest

Even if the people around you do not rebel, you are doomed to reap what you have sown. Galatians 6:7 will work against your good preaching, good principles, handsome appearance and clever strategies. It is just a matter of time. It may take ten years but the Scripture cannot be broken.

In the case of Absalom, he reaped what he had sown almost immediately. In his very first cabinet meeting, he was mistakenly led to choose a disloyal person as his chief counselor.

God had determined to destroy Absalom and the Lord worked it out by making Absalom choose a disloyal person's advice.

Ahithophel had been part of the conspiracy for months and maybe even years. Hushai, the Archite, was actually a loyal friend of David who had been planted in Absalom's camp to mislead him. Absalom knew that the two wisest men whose advice his father had trusted were Hushai the Archite and Ahithophel the Gilonite.

Can you believe that Absalom chose to reject the counsel of his long-standing and loyal conspirator, Ahithophel, on that fateful night? This is the only thing that made Absalom lose the battle. He chose a disloyal person as his right-hand man

Hushai: The Harvest of Absalom's Disloyalty

For they have sown the wind, and they shall REAP THE WHIRLWIND...

Hosea 8:7

If you are an "Absalom", God will make you choose evil because you have been evil to someone. You will unknowingly select wicked and unfaithful people. Liars and thieves will dance in circles around you. Your money will never be enough because the people that count and manage it will steal from you constantly.

Treacherous women, more bitter than death, will be sent to destroy your life. Mercy! This is one of the punishments of God: "And I find more bitter than death the woman, whose heart is snares and nets, and her hands as bands: whoso pleaseth God shall escape from her; but the sinner shall be taken by her" (Ecclesiastes 7:26).

Wizards will be your accountants. You will unwittingly employ witches to assist you in the ministry. This is because when you were employed, you were a witch and a wizard to your employer. *Anytime there is a choice between a good person and a bad person, you will choose the bad person.* You will choose the wrong husband and the wrong wife. It will be a punishment and a snare to you for the rest of your days because you are not a loyal person.

If there is a good car and a defective car, you will always choose the defective one because when you were chosen you were evil to the one who chose you. If there is a good man and a bad man, you will always prefer the bad one. You will desire evil things and choose snares and traps for yourself because you were a snare to someone who loved you. You will reap a hundredfold of your disloyalty and treachery! He that sows the wind will reap the whirlwind!

Many people do not realize that even the people you work with and lean on are gifts from God. *Absalom had the best options but he was doomed to choose the wrong thing.* Because he himself was a "wrong" child to his father.

I always pray that God will lead me to choose good people who will not harm me. Reaping and sowing are eternal principles of God's Word. Anyone who claims to be working for God must respect that law.

Chapter 3

Bad Advisors

Every purpose is established by counsel: and with good advice make war.

Proverbs 20:18

Every leader must surround himself with loyal people. Some of these people will become counselors. The counsel of the people around you will make a lot of difference. The Scripture shows us that purposes are established through good counsel. What God has decided to do with your life will only be accomplished with wise counsel.

Ministers who depend solely on supernatural things usually do not do well. This is because we operate both in natural and spiritual dimensions. Large aspects of what we will do in the ministry will involve the natural and the physical.

Legal advice, medical advice and technical advice in various fields are crucial to success in ministry. We need the anointing but we also need natural wisdom.

We need both the power and the wisdom of God. I dare say much of the failure in ministry comes about through the absence of good advice.

Things Work Together

The Bible teaches that *all things* work together for good. This means that several things work in tandem to produce a certain result. In the New Testament, people were chosen because they had several gifts and abilities which worked together to make them who they were. Stephen was a man full of the Spirit and full of faith. "And they chose Stephen, a man full of faith and of the Holy Spirit" (Acts 6:5 NASU).

Barnabas was also described as a man full of the Spirit and full of faith. "For he was a good man, and full of the Holy Spirit and of faith" (Acts 11:24 NASU).

They did not just have the Holy Spirit. They also had faith. The seven helpers who were chosen to assist the apostles had a good reputation, the Holy Spirit and wisdom. These three things worked together to make them successful helps ministers. "Select from among you seven men of good reputation, full of the Spirit and of wisdom, whom we may put in charge of this task" (Acts 6:3). Let's get back to our discussion on advisors who make a difference for the ministry.

The Search for Loyal Advisors

The counsel of Hushai the Archite is better than the counsel of Ahithophel."

2 Samuel 17:14 (NASU)

Many times you cannot tell whether the advice of one person is better than the other. Most ministers do not have the ability to understand and relate with different subjects and fields of learning. Some ministers have no idea about legal things and so have to depend on the input of others.

Think of the legal, architectural, accounting, engineering, financial, human resource, computer and even medical aspects of life which affect your life. How can you be successful if you did not have the right advice in any of these fields?

I always remember the story of the prophet Branham who was the most humble and simple of the healing evangelists, having and owning very little. However, he was the one who was taken to court for tax issues and owed the state until he died. Obviously, the people who surrounded him and advised him in these areas did not protect and help him.

Then Absalom and all the men of Israel said, "THE COUNSEL OF HUSHAI THE ARCHITE IS BETTER THAN THE COUNSEL OF AHITHOPHEL." For the LORD had ordained to thwart the good counsel of Ahithophel, so that the LORD might bring calamity on Absalom.

2 Samuel 17:14 (NASU)

Absalom set out to become the king of Israel. He almost succeeded in this quest but failed because he followed wrong advice. In the Scripture above, Absalom declared that the advice of Hushai was better than the advice of Ahithophel. But was it really better?

Absalom's plan had taken years to develop. His plan worked beautifully until he followed wrong advice. In this chapter, I want to give you a few ideas on how to identify loyal men and good counselors. May God save you from disloyal men! God will bless you with good advice through loyal men who love you.

Seven Keys to Obtaining Good Counsel

1. Choose someone who has been with you for a long time.

Absalom had two options: he had to choose between the advice of Ahithophel the Gillonite and the advice of Hushai the Archite. He made the crucial mistake of choosing Hushai as his advisor even though Ahithophel's advice was the best advice he could have had. "And the counsel of Ahithophel, which he counseled in those days, was as if a man had inquired at the oracle of God: *so was all the counsel of Ahithophel both with David and with Absalom*" (2 Samuel 16:23).

Indeed, the advice of Ahithophel to Absalom was like the superior wisdom of God. But why was Absalom confused? Why did he make the mistake of choosing the advice of Hushai the Archite instead of taking the advice of Ahithophel the Gilonite?

The truth about counsel is that there are many ways to do the same thing. Each method and each suggestion has pros and cons. It is not always easy to know which way is better. Sometimes, it does seem impossible to distinguish between good and bad advice.

Ahithophel's Plan

Ahithophel presented Absalom with a good plan that promised to wipe out his father, David, forever. "Furthermore, Ahithophel said to Absalom, "Please let me choose 12,000 men that I may arise and pursue David tonight.

I will come upon him while he is weary and exhausted and terrify him, so that all the people who are with him will flee. Then I will strike down the king alone, and I will bring back all the people to you. The return of everyone depends on the man you seek; then all the people will be at peace."

So the plan pleased Absalom and all the elders of Israel" (2 Samuel 17:1-4 NASU).

Hushai's Plan

Hushai also presented Absalom with an equally good plan, which had great promise of victory. "So Hushai said to Absalom, "This time the advice that Ahithophel has given is not good."

Moreover, Hushai said, "You know your father and his men, that they are mighty men and they are fierce, like a bear robbed of her cubs in the field. And your father is an expert in warfare, and will not spend the night with the people. Behold, he has now hidden himself in one of the caves or in another place; and it will be when he falls on them at the first attack, that whoever hears it will say, 'There has been a slaughter among the people who follow Absalom.' And even the one who is valiant, whose heart is like the heart of a lion, will completely lose heart; for all Israel knows that your father is a mighty man and those who are with him are valiant men.

But I counsel that all Israel be surely gathered to you, from Dan even to Beersheba, as the sand that is by the sea in abundance, and that you personally go into battle. So we shall come to him in one of the places where he can be found, and we will fall on him as the dew falls on the ground; and of him and of all the men who are with him, not even one will be left.

And if he withdraws into a city, then all Israel shall bring ropes to that city, and we will drag it into the valley until not even a small stone is found there" (2 Samuel 17:7-13 NASU).

Which Plan Was Better?

As you can see both plans sound good and few people would have been able to distinguish the good from the bad.

However, one principle could have saved Absalom; the principle of preferring a loyal person's input to the advice of someone of unproven loyalties. Absalom should have chosen to listen to the advice of someone whose loyalty was guaranteed.

Ahithophel was a long-standing supporter of the conspiracy to overthrow King David. Absalom actually sent for Ahithophel when it was time to overthrow King David. He was the person Absalom should have listened to.

Absalom would have been safer with anything that Ahithophel proposed because he had already proved that he was on his side. "And Absalom sent for Ahithophel the Gilonite, David's counselor, from his city Giloh, while he was offering the sacrifices. And the conspiracy was strong, for the people increased continually with Absalom" (2 Samuel 15:12).

The advice of Hushai was lengthier and more impressive. It involved more options and counter proposals in case anything went wrong. Ahithophel's advice was brief and not as impressive as Hushai's. Unfortunately, many people listen to new and flashy counselors rather than depending on old faithful people whose loyalties have been proven over the years.

This is a fatal mistake and it is on this very point that many ministries and even businesses begin a downward spiral. I prefer to listen to old faithful people who have demonstrated that they love me and believe in me.

2. *Follow the advice of someone who is prepared to implement it himself.*

Follow the advice of someone who is prepared to implement what he is suggesting. Absalom failed to recognize this. If he had known this, he would have chosen to listen to Ahithophel rather than to Hushai. There are people who give advice but will not help to carry it out. In fact, they have no idea about how to carry out their own instructions.

Ahithophel made a suggestion and offered to carry it out himself. That was significant. "Moreover Ahithophel said unto Absalom, **LET ME** now choose out twelve thousand men, and **I WILL ARISE** and pursue after David this night: And **I WILL COME** upon him while he is weary and weak handed, and will make him afraid: and all the people that are with him shall flee; and **I WILL SMITE** the king only: And **I WILL BRING** back all the people unto thee: the man whom thou seekest is as if all returned: so all the people shall be in peace. And the saying pleased Absalom well, and all the elders of Israel" (2 Samuel 17:1-4).

But notice that the advice that Hushai the Archite gave. First of all, he never offered to help Absalom carry out the plan. He rather advised Absalom to endanger himself by going out into battle himself.

Unfortunately, Absalom could not see that he was being sent to his own death. "But I counsel that all Israel be surely gathered to you, from Dan even to Beersheba, as the sand that is by the sea in abundance, and that **YOU PERSONALLY GO INTO BATTLE**" (2Samuel 17:11 NASU).

Anytime I receive a suggestion, I often ask the person suggesting it to carry it out himself. That is how to determine if advice is usable or not.

Unfortunately, many people are not practical and cannot build anything. They may have certificates from school, but they cannot translate what they have learnt in school into reality.

Many churches are run by priests with theological certificates. However, these certificates do not help the church to grow. Likewise, many nations are run by theoreticians with university degrees. Unfortunately, a degree from school means very little when it comes to real nation building.

You must learn to distinguish between people who talk a lot with high-sounding ideas and people who bring practical solutions. Surround yourself with people who solve problems and make things happen practically.

Bad Advisors

3. *Do not follow advice that is based on fear.*

Hushai was a wise man and he knew he had to frighten Absalom away from the path of success. Hushai's advice incited much fear. Hushai spoke of several things that frightened Absalom and his followers.

He reminded Absalom and the other rebellious elders that David was a very experienced soldier - a winner of many battles. He asked Absalom to remember the kind of person his father was. He described David as a bear. And not an ordinary bear, but a female bear robbed of her cubs! That is not an animal anyone would like to meet!

Moreover, Hushai said, "You know your father and his men, that they are mighty men and they are fierce, like a bear robbed of her cubs in the field. And your father is an expert in warfare...

2 Samuel 17:8 (NASU)

He also reminded them of the kind of mighty men that were with David. A list of these mighty men in 2 Samuel 23 would send chills down the spine of any brave warrior. Hushai told Absalom to watch out for terrible fighters like Joab the commander and Abishai, his brother, who killed three hundred men in one go.

Hushai reminded Absalom of Adino the Eznite, who killed eight hundred people at one time. Then he told him not to forget about Benaiah the son of Jehoiada, who killed a lion in the middle of a pit on a snowy day.

What about Abishai, who killed Goliath's brother?

After listening to an unsettling account of these mighty men, Absalom was frightened. This same thing happened to the children of Israel just before they entered the Promised Land. They heard of the giants and were frightened away from the Promised Land.

They backed off from their God-given heritage because of the frightening details they heard. You will never do well as long as you listen to advice that inspires fear.

Listen to Can-Do Advice

Ahithophel's advice was "can-do" advice! It was positive! It was practical! It was possibility thinking. It was advice that could be followed immediately. Most things that can be done can be done *now*!

Let's Marry Right Now!

Years ago, when I met my wife, I told her that I wanted to marry her *immediately*. I really desired to marry her as soon as practical. I felt that I had made up my mind and there was no more reason to delay. "Let's get on with it and get married!"

I thought she would be unsettled by my insistence on us marrying soon. But she wasn't. One day, she told me something that surprised me.

She said, "My father says, 'If a man will really marry you, he will want to marry you right now.'

Through experience, her father would identify good young suitors by their desire to marry at once.

Now, in my own experience, I have noticed that men who say, "I will marry you in the next four years'", "I will marry

Bad Advisors

you when I come back from my five year post-graduate program", do not usually get married as promised.

Always remember that advice that can be implemented immediately is usually good advice.

4. *Follow advice that brings peace and strength.*

Ahithophel's advice was based on his understanding of human behavior. He wanted Absalom to do things that would encourage the troops. He knew that the psychological strength of the people on the mission would make or break them.

Ahithophel wanted Absalom to sleep with his father's wives so that his rebellious troops would sense the determination of a resolute leader and be strengthened by it.

"Then Absalom said to Ahithophel, "Give your advice. What shall we do?" Ahithophel said to Absalom, "Go in to your father's concubines, whom he has left to keep the house; then all Israel will hear that you have made yourself odious to your father. THE HANDS OF ALL WHO ARE WITH YOU WILL ALSO BE STRENGTHENED So they pitched a tent for Absalom on the roof, and Absalom went in to his father's concubines in the sight of all Israel" (2Samuel 16:20-22 NASU).

When Ahithophel suggested that Absalom sleep with his father's wives, it was not because he wanted Absalom to taste King David's exclusive and exquisite sexual delights. This was certainly not the time for relaxation or sexual pleasure. It was time for boosting the morale of the troops. It was time to win the confidence of the troops and to succeed in their mission. It was time to let the troops know that they were following a strong, determined and fearless leader!

The next bit of Ahithophel's advice was also based on the concept of strengthening and stabilizing his followers.

...and I will bring back all the people to you. The return of everyone depends on the man you seek; THEN ALL THE PEOPLE WILL BE AT PEACE."

2 Samuel 17:3 (NASU)

You cannot build a church unless the people following you have peace and a sense of well-being. You must do things that make them feel strengthened in their mission. If the people who follow you have no sense of security, they will soon give up.

Years ago, I was the leader of a small group of students, which was developing into a church. When it became apparent that I did not intend to leave the country or the church, the people who followed me were strengthened and became more committed. The church grew and became established. We grew out of our little classroom and became a mega church.

Building a team of full-time workers and missionaries will require much of Ahithophel's kind of wisdom. Without peace and a sense of well-being, people will constantly abandon ship.

There is something that I call "*a feel well item*". I have learned over the years that the administration of these "*feel well items*" dramatically boosts the morale of the troops. Every leader should learn to do things that bring encouragement, peace and well-being to his followers. The "feel well" environment is not created by splashing money around. The Holy Spirit will have to guide you into this kind of wisdom.

People have remarked about the number of medical doctors, engineers, lawyers, gold miners and highly qualified people who have abandoned their jobs to follow me into ministry. These people work for me willingly for a small fraction of what they would have earned in the world. I have watched as highly paid professionals in USA and Europe abandoned what they were doing, came to Africa and worked for virtually nothing.

I do not have much money to offer them but they seem to be eager and blessed to work in the ministry. This is not my doing because I did not plan or engineer it. Looking back however, I realize how God's grace has brought about the Ahithophel kind of wisdom to make his will possible.

5. *Follow advice that accomplishes one thing at a time.*

Ahithophel's plan hinged on targeting one person, King David. This is an eternal principle that guarantees success in almost any endeavor. Ahithophel tried to explain that the outcome of the entire operation depended on taking on one person.

Pastors will accomplish more if they target the right people. Ministering to large numbers and targeting multitudes is great. However, if you want real growth you will have to focus on a few individuals who can fulfil the vision.

"...and I will bring back all the people to you. The return of everyone DEPENDS ON THE MAN YOU SEEK; then all the people will be at peace." (2 Samuel 17:3 NASU)

Many people feel that strength comes from targeting large numbers.

Ahithophel targeted only one man, King David. Hushai suggested that they eliminate David *and* all the men that were with him. Ahithophel targeted one person and Hushai targeted the multitude of mighty men.

This grandiose idea sounded more promising as it would get rid of all the mighty men who were loyal to David. "So we shall come to him in one of the places where he can be found, and we will fall on him as the dew falls on the ground; and OF HIM AND OF ALL THE MEN WHO ARE WITH HIM, NOT EVEN ONE WILL BE LEFT" '(2 Samuel 17:12 NASU). How impressive! Not even one of David's mighty men would have been left if this plan had been executed.

When King David fought back at Absalom, this principle was taken into account and David was not allowed to go into the battle. They told him, 'if they even kill half of us, it will not matter, but if *you* die, that will be the end of all of us. "And the king said to the people, "I myself will surely go out with you also." But the people said, "You should not go out; for if we indeed flee, they will not care about us; even if half of us die, they will not care about us. But you are worth ten thousand of us; therefore now it is better that you be ready to help us from the city."'(2 Samuel 18:2-3 NASU).

Now, this was a war between David's army and Absalom's army. Absalom followed the bad advice of Hushai to go out himself whilst David followed good advice and stayed at home. Simply put, this became a war between the wise and the foolish.

Just as Ahithophel predicted, the war ended when one man was killed. And Absalom was the one man whose death ended the war! Ahithophel knew that everything hinged on what happened to one person. "And ten young men who carried Joab's armor gathered around and struck Absalom and killed him. Then Joab blew the trumpet, and the people returned from pursuing Israel, for Joab restrained the people" (2 Samuel 18:15-16 NASU). As soon as Absalom was dead, the conflict was over.

Perhaps, it is this principle that most of us fail to see. If we were able to reach the one person that God has called us to, we would accomplish much more. Because we love the pomp and fame that come with doing programs with groups, we do not spend time on the individuals who can make all the difference.

Every leader should do what it takes to build his ministry. Do what you have to do! Spend time with the few you need to spend time with. Many people's lives depend on your ability to choose a few key people and invest in them. Make some people special because that is the reality. They are special to your life and to your survival!

The devil seems to know the wisdom of Ahithophel better than most Christians. That is why he attacks believers one at a time. He is not so worried about the church you belong to. He will take you up when you are alone. "Be sober, be vigilant; because your adversary the devil, as a roaring lion, walketh about, seeking whom he may devour" (1 Peter 5:8).

Lions hunt down their prey one at a time. You will never find a lion targeting seventeen antelopes at the same time.

Satan Targets Individuals One at a Time

Satan is seeking to destroy key leaders on whom much depends. You may look weak when you don't do certain things. A leader may look wasteful when certain amounts of money are spent on him.

I am sure that some accused Absalom of being a coward for not going into battle himself. Nevertheless, he was a fool to go and it cost him his life when he went.

Sometimes, the difficulties you go through as a person are because of the position of leadership you are in. If you were not occupying that all-important chair, you would not experience one tenth of your current problems.

There are financial problems that will beset you because you are in that special position.

The media will harass you because of your position in the ministry.

There are serious marital problems that may plague you just because of your role in the ministry. I have watched pastors who have had beautiful marriages begin to have serious problems when they became senior pastors.

Higher levels usually attract higher devils. Kings and 'immortal" leaders have died because they were the sole target of almost every attack.

Ahab, the famous husband of Jezebel, fought a battle in which he was the sole target. That is the battle that ended his life!

> **And the king of Israel said unto Jehoshaphat, I will disguise myself, and enter into the battle; but put thou on thy robes. And the king of Israel disguised himself, and went into the battle. But the king of Syria commanded his thirty and two captains that had rule over his chariots, saying, FIGHT NEITHER WITH SMALL NOR GREAT, SAVE ONLY WITH THE KING of Israel. And it came to pass, when the captains of the chariots saw**

Jehoshaphat, that they said, Surely it is the king of Israel. And they turned aside to fight against him: and Jehoshaphat cried out. And it came to pass, when the captains of the chariots perceived that it was not the king of Israel, that they turned back from pursuing him. And a certain man drew a bow at a venture, and smote the king of Israel between the joints of the harness:'

1 Kings 22:30-34

Ahab was the sole target of that war. The king or leader is the light of the group he leads. David was called the light of Israel and that was why he was treated specially. "But Abishai the son of Zeruiah succoured him, and smote the Philistine, and killed him. Then the men of David sware unto him, saying, Thou shalt go no more out with us to battle, that thou quench not the light of Israel" (2 Samuel 21:17).

Never forget that the leader is the light of the group he leads. If the light is quenched, darkness will descend on everyone that follows him.

6. *Follow advice that is implemented through one person.*

I believe that many things can be accomplished through one key person. Achieving goals through groups, committees and large numbers of people is an attractive option to some people.

But I have experienced much success by working with one key person on every project. God's Word shows us that he searches for one person and works through one person. "And I sought for A MAN among them, that should make up the hedge, and stand in the gap before me for the land, that I should not destroy it: but I found none" (Ezekiel 22:30).

Absalom wanted to know what both Ahithophel and Hushai thought on the matter. Both advisors spoke and once again, Absalom had two options to choose from.

Hushai, who was intentionally giving bad advice told Absalom to work through *thousands* of people. "But I COUNSEL THAT ALL ISRAEL BE SURELY GATHERED TO YOU, from Dan even to Beersheba, as the sand that is by the sea in abundance, and that you personally go into battle" (2 Samuel 17:11).

Ahithophel however offered to seek out the king and eliminate him personally. "Ahithophel said to Absalom, Please let me choose 12,000 men that I MAY arise and pursue David tonight. I WILL come upon him while he is weary and exhausted and terrify him, so that all the people who are with him will flee. Then I WILL strike down the king alone" (2 Samuel 17:1-2 NASU).

Can you see why Absalom would prefer Hushai's advice? Hushai's plan was to fight a war with thousands and thousands of people who numbered like the sand of the sea. Ahithophel's plan involved only twelve thousand men and him personally assassinating King David.

Unfortunately, Absalom opted to accomplish his purpose through large numbers of people. I can see how working with larger groups is more attractive. Preaching to big congregations gives you the feeling that you are doing more.

Somehow, Jesus seemed to think otherwise; that is why he spent more time with his disciples than with the large crowds. He knew that everything depended on one person. That is why He said, "It is written, I will smite the shepherd, and the sheep of the flock shall be scattered abroad" (Matthew 26:31).

Most of the teachings that we read from the book of John were given to the small group of disciples. From the fifth chapter of John, Jesus' focused his ministry on the twelve disciples and not on the multitudes.

God has blessed me with individuals through whom I work. I am engaged in different unrelated areas of ministry. However, I tackle each area through the help of just one person. Whatever I build, I do through one person. I do not attempt to build a church unless I have one man - the pastor. If I want to have a mission to a foreign nation, all I need is one person - the missionary. I do not depend on getting the commitment and approval of several people.

I need only one person to establish a new department. I do not depend on teams or groups. This has worked best for me. That is the Ahithophel kind of wisdom which is also the oracle of God for you!

Years ago, I established a music group called "The BeeDees". I wanted to build a wonderful team of musicians who would sing and play together. After a while, everyone went in different directions and the group disintegrated. I was very disappointed to say the least. However, I realized that I could never accomplish my vision for music through a group. Now, I work with individuals and that is working better.

7. *Follow advice that is based on good timing.*

A crucial aspect of Ahithophel's plan was to attack David at the right time.

King David was a strong fighter but he was not invincible neither was he immortal. Naturally, given the right conditions, King David could be defeated. Ahithophel knew exactly when and how David could be defeated and he said so.

"Ahithophel said to Absalom, Please let me choose 12,000 men that I may arise and pursue David TONIGHT" (2Samuel 17:1 NASU).

The key word here is *"tonight"*. It was important that Absalom pursue David at that particular time. Ahithophel knew that conditions were favorable *only for that night*.

What conditions made that night favorable for Absalom?

David was weary and exhausted and Ahithophel wanted the attack to come on during David's lowest moment "I will come upon him WHILE HE IS WEARY AND EXHAUSTED and terrify him, so that all the people who are with him will flee. Then I will strike down the king alone" (2 Samuel 17:2).

Hushai also knew that David was weary and exhausted and he wanted to buy some time for David. That is why he asked him to wait until thousands and thousands of troops could gather. Can you imagine how long it took to assemble all these troops?

The Right Timing

Dear friend, there is a time to every purpose. If you miss the timing, you are not likely to succeed. Whilst you are on this earth, everything you do will depend on doing it at the right time.

God may have chosen you to have the largest church in your country. But perhaps, the right time to begin this great ministry is when you are twenty-five years old. If you delay and begin when you are forty-five years old, the vision will be greatly affected. Wrong timing makes things look as though it is not God's will. Many times it is the will of God but the wrong time.

Ahithophel advised Absalom to attack when David was tired. He knew that Absalom's only chance was when his father was physically exhausted.

Why was Ahithophel's advice better than Hushai's? Because Ahithophel's advice took into account *the right time* for accomplishing the vision.

Strength through Camps

There are battles that every strong leader will lose just because he is exhausted. That is why God wants us to have retreats and camps to strengthen ourselves. Your ministry will be transformed when you have camps.

David had a camp at a place called Mahanaim and the camp director was Barzillai, the Gileadite. "And Israel and Absalom camped in the land of Gilead. Now when David had come to Mahanaim, Shobi the son of Nahash from Rabbah of the sons of Ammon, Machir the son of Ammiel from Lodebar, and Barzillai the Gileadite from Rogelim, brought beds, basins, pottery, wheat, barley, flour, parched grain, beans, lentils, parched seeds, honey, curds, sheep, and cheese of the herd, for David and for the people who were with him, to eat; for they said, "The people are hungry and weary and thirsty in the wilderness."' (2 Sam 17:26-29). "Now Barzillai was very old, being eighty years old; and he had sustained the king while he stayed at Mahanaim, for he was a very great man" (2 Samuel 19:32). Later on, King David rewarded Barzillai the Gileadite for his help in refreshing them.

Absalom gave David enough time to rest and to eat bread, beans, meat, honey etc. By the time Absalom got his act together, Barzillai, the Gileadite had brought him all the food, basins and beds that he needed.

Don't try fighting David after he has eaten bread, cheese, beans, parched grain and beef. It was a fatal mistake to take on David's mighty men after they had eaten. It was simply the wrong time to fight someone like David and his mighty men. Absalom should have fought them when they were tired and hungry. He missed the right time and lost everything.

Can you imagine the strength that Adino the Eznite, a killer of eight hundred people would have after eating a whole sheep? Can you imagine how strong Abishai, the killer of Goliath's brother would have felt after eating a whole goat?

It is important that you understand that success and failure depend greatly on timing. May the Holy Spirit guide you into knowing the time for his purposes. Absalom failed because he attacked David at the wrong time. Which part of your ministry is failing because of poor timing?

Do not set yourself up for discouragement by embarking on things that you are not ready for.

Do not launch out into fields that are not ripened for harvest.

Chapter 4

Painfully Disloyal People

My heart is sore pained within me.

Psalm 55:4

King David lamented over Ahithophel in the fifty-fifth psalm. It is believed that he wrote this psalm about Ahithophel, his special friend and counselor. Ahithophel turned against David and caused him much pain. Ahithophel was David's special friend and counselor, but one fateful night he turned against his friend and offered to be the leader who would kill the king. "Furthermore, Ahithophel said to Absalom, "Please let me choose 12,000 men that I may arise and pursue David tonight" (2 Samuel 17:1 NASU).

In this Psalm, he pours out his heart and tells us the pain he experienced through betrayal. It is a very painful thing to experience betrayal. Many ministers do not recover from their experiences with treachery.

Disloyalty can break your heart and your ministry. It can sow the seeds of bitterness in the heart of someone who had a sweet spirit.

Derek Prince Regrets

In his last interview, Derek Prince was asked if he had any regrets. He spoke about one regret. He wished he had been more forgiving. He mentioned a painful experience with painful people, which he had found difficult to forget.

You will notice how older ministers tend to be hardened and not so trusting. A certain sweetness is found in younger people who have never experienced betrayal. Those who have never been betrayed do not understand all this talk about loyalty. Initially, I was upset when ministers criticized my book 'Loyalty and Disloyalty". But after a while, I realized that most of these ministers were not experienced in certain things. They had never had certain types of crises before. Like many things, it is difficult to imagine something you have never experienced.

He Did Not Understand

One Pastor said to me, "Why should you bother to teach about loyalty?"

He continued, "Loyalty is not something that is taught. It is something you earn."

He went further, "You command respect, you don't teach it." He made light of my book and dismissed it.

However, a few years later, this person became a chief proponent of the loyalty doctrine. He taught from my book and recommended it to other ministers. He even jokingly offered to become a salesman for my book on loyalty and disloyalty. What brought about the change? What had happened to make my friend turn around so drastically? Experience! Experience with treacherous people like Ahithophel!

Another minister dismissed my teaching on loyalty and disloyalty as being frivolous and unnecessary. He said many bad things about my work. But one day, his right-hand man did to him what Ahithophel did to David.

He could not believe what happened to him. Several of his pastors turned against him and resigned. Just like David, his heart was broken and he could not bear to stay in his own church anymore. He did not love his people anymore and wanted to be away from them as much as possible.

My Experiences with Disloyalty

1. A Feeling of Abandonment

Give ear to my prayer, O God; and hide not thyself from my supplication. Attend unto me, and hear me: I mourn in my complaint, and make a noise

Psalm 55:1-2

Experiences with disloyal people will make you pray harder. There is a sense of being forgotten by God. You will feel like praying because the experience of betrayal is very sobering. That is why David said, "...Don't hide yourself from my prayer."

A Bad Dream

Years ago, one of my trusted pastors turned against me in a very painful way. I prayed, prayed, and wondered where God was. It was my first experience and probably the nastiest so far. The only thing I could compare it to was a bad dream. Actually, I remember making a particular comment repeatedly.

I said, "If I had had a bad dream, I would never have dreamt that this could happen. My mind would have rejected the dream." You know how it is when in a dream, you are being chased and you somehow wake up before you actually die or are eaten by the lion. Somehow, your mind refuses bad things, even in a dream! My experience with painfully disloyal people was so terrible that I realized that even my dreamy head would reject the experience.

2. Intolerable Accusations

Because of the voice of the enemy, because of the oppression of the wicked: for THEY CAST INIQUITY UPON ME, and in wrath they hate me. My heart is sore pained within me: and the terrors of death are fallen upon me

Psalm 55:3-4

One of the terrible aspects of disloyalty is the intolerable accusations that are brought against you by treacherous and disloyal men.

David said, "They cast iniquity upon me."

Disloyal people attribute all kinds of sins to you.

When you hear what is said about you, you would wonder whether you are Satan or his representative. Somehow, these accusations work on you and are extremely painful. Intolerable accusers re-describe events and fabricate half-truths that make you look terrible. All these accusations come from people you have known, loved and trusted.

I remember the intolerable accusations of a pastor whom I sent on a mission. At a meeting before he left, he was given a briefing and some instructions. As part of his briefing, he was told about the different people he would be dealing with so that he would know how to conduct himself. With the passage of time, this brother left our ministry in anger and moved on to do other things.

One day, he had the chance to interact again with some of the people he had been briefed about earlier. He recounted to some of them a distorted version of what he had been told. He told a particular woman that she was a topic for discussion amongst pastors and that we considered her to be very immoral.

This lady was aghast. "Is that what they said?" She asked.

He smiled and told her, 'They told me you are a 'wild fornicator'. You have no idea what they say about you." He then told them how I was a thief, stealing the church's money and enriching myself. He gave them evidence and showed them exactly how I went about my stealing. The next time I interacted with that community, I received a hostile response. An intolerable accuser had walked through the church, spreading his poison, *re-presenting and re-describing* everything he knew. From then on, it was very difficult to function in that church. Many of the people this fellow spoke with left the ministry in disgust. Perhaps, their souls will be lost through the hard work of this accusing friend.

King David said, "... they cast iniquity upon me." That is exactly what a disloyal person does. He throws sins at you that you have not committed. Sadly, a whole lot of negative stuff will be attributed to you.

3. Fears of Desolation

My heart is sore pained within me: and the terrors of death are fallen upon me. FEARFULNESS AND TREMBLING ARE COME UPON ME, and horror hath overwhelmed me

Psalm 55:4-5

One of the things that happened to me was the fear of failure and desolation. When someone spreads bad stories about you, it is difficult to believe that God can still use you.

It is difficult to believe that your ministry will work in spite of bad impressions that people have about you. How can anyone ever believe in a thief? How can anyone believe in someone so evil?

Somehow, you think that your church will never grow again.

One individual threatened me and said, "I will run you out of town."

I truly felt that I could be run out of town. Will you survive the desperate accusations that are hurled against you?

My heart missed a beat when he said, "I will publish a book about you."

This is how David felt when Ahithophel and the men of Israel turned on him. He said, "Fearfulness and trembling are come upon me." King David thought his reign was over. He felt all his successes had ended. His blessed reign as king had crumbled and everything was over. But it is not over until God says it is over!

4. The Desire to Be Far from Disloyal People

And I said, OH THAT I HAD WINGS LIKE A DOVE! FOR THEN WOULD I FLY AWAY, AND BE AT REST. Lo, then would I wander far off, and remain in the wilderness. Selah. I would hasten my escape from the windy storm and tempest.

Psalm 55:6-8 (NASU)

One of the strange things that happen after experiencing disloyalty is a desire to be very far from treacherous people.

Years ago, a pastor resigned from my ministry and visited some of our church members. He visited various families he had known whilst in the ministry. Amongst other things, he told them that it was only the crocodile who could tell what was going on under the river. He explained how he had lived under the river for a long time and knew all the goings-on there. He was also well acquainted with the other "creatures"'that dwelled under the river.

He explained, "I have worked at the highest level of the ministry and so I know what is really going on up there."

When I heard the details of how evil I was, I felt awful and almost ashamed of myself.

There is something about accusations that makes you want to fly away. As King David said in Psalm 55, "Oh that I had wings like a dove! for then would I fly away, and be at rest."

This dear brother pointed to a new car that I had just acquired and explained to the unsuspecting members how I had looted the church's coffers to greedily acquire it.

By the time this brother had finished spreading his stories, I did not feel like visiting that church anymore. Like a dove, I wanted to fly away and be at rest. I wanted to be as far as possible from the disloyal brother and the people he had poisoned.

One time when I did visit this group, I could not think of what to preach about. I was so uncomfortable in the church because I did not feel welcome.

As I sat in the front row, I wondered, "What should I preach about?" I opened my Bible at random and my eyes fell on a strange verse that I had not seen before.

The righteous also shall hold on his way, and he that hath clean hands shall be stronger and stronger.

Job 17:9

"What a strange verse," I thought, but I decided to use it as my text.

The eyes of the congregation were fixed on me. They had heard all the bad stories about me and were waiting to hear from me. There was silence in the church as I preached that Sunday morning.

I told the church that I would hold onto my course of preaching the gospel and planting churches.

Then I explained that if I had clean hands, I would only get stronger and stronger in the ministry.

"Time will tell everything," I concluded.

Before I took my seat, I had one more thing to do.

This church had attempted to put together some money to buy me a present. Somehow, they had not yet been able to obtain the targeted amount. I announced to them that the gift they wanted to purchase for me was well-appreciated but not necessary anymore. I pointed out that their money was not enough to pay for even half of the cost of the intended gift.

That morning, I returned their money to them asking them to either donate it to the church or take it back. Some of them took their money back and others donated it to the church. Then I knelt down before the congregation, and asked them to forgive me for any wrong I had done against them and to receive back their gifts.

I honestly did not enjoy preaching in that church and never really have, since then. Somehow, there was a feeling, which David described in the Scripture above "LO THEN WOULD I WANDER FAR OFF, AND REMAIN IN THE WILDERNESS."

Years went by and my busy schedule gave me more reasons to avoid such a group of suspicious church members.

One day, I had a vision. In the vision, I found myself flying in a helicopter. After a while I noticed that the helicopter was landing somewhere.

I looked out of the window to see where we were landing. To my surprise, we were landing in one of these church members' house.

I was so surprised because it was the last place I would have landed my helicopter.

Then the Lord said to me, "It's time to go back and visit these people again." It took a supernatural revelation to make me go back there.

I Can't Take Ingratitude

After experiencing a rebellion from an assistant pastor, one senior pastor said to us, "I cannot stay in my church for more than two weeks in a row."

He explained, "I am very sensitive and everything I do, I do from my heart."

He continued, "It is a very difficult thing for me to pour out my heart and to love people, only for them to turn on me."

"I can't take such ingratitude."

You see, he was experiencing what David experienced! He had joined David in saying "*Lo then would I wander far off, and remain in the wilderness.*" Pastors, you will have to learn to swallow ingratitude and disloyalty with the love of God. It is part of real life and ministry.

5. The Contradiction of Sinners

DESTROY, O LORD, AND DIVIDE THEIR TONGUES: for I have seen violence and strife in the city. Day and night, they go about it upon the walls thereof: mischief also and sorrow are in the midst of it. Wickedness is in the midst thereof: deceit and guile depart not from her streets.

Psalm 55:9-11

King David prayed about the things that his friend Ahithophel was saying and doing. He asked God to confound and contradict everything about Ahithophel. And David said, "O LORD, I pray, make the counsel of Ahithophel foolishness." (2 Samuel 15:31) "Confuse, O Lord, divide their tongues" (Psalm 55:9).

I have watched as this Scripture has been literally fulfilled. God can make people that criticize you look foolish. God can confound the tongues of your enemies and that is what David prayed for.

I remember a young, rebellious pastor who went around trying to get some key church members to leave my ministry and join him.

He gave this particular brother several reasons why I was not fit to be in the ministry and why he should leave my ministry.

I asked, "What exactly did he say about me?"

Apparently, he had told the brother many damaging stories about me.

He gave me some details and remarked that the pastor had been very passionate and convincing.

However, before I could even react he said, "But I didn't believe a word of what he said."

He continued, "I could see right through him.'

He added, "The hatred and the venom were so evident."

I was surprised at the way this brother was not taken in by my rebellious friend. After all, he had heard enough to make him want to leave. But, somehow, God turns the hearts of some people against rebellious people. He exposes the hypocrisy for what it truly is.

It is amazing that in spite of the numerous, slanderous stories about God's men they continue to flourish and preach the gospel. This is what David prayed for. "Let the wisdom and the words of Ahithophel look foolish!" This was King David's prayer, "Destroy, O Lord, and divide their tongues."

6. Feelings of Vengeance

Let death seize upon them, and let them go down quick into hell: for wickedness is in their dwellings, and among them

Psalm 55:15

Betrayal provokes hateful feelings against the traitor. King David wanted the disloyal people around him to die and go to hell immediately. In the army, traitors are quickly executed.

Anyone who tries to overthrow a government is immediately dealt with and often pays the highest penalty for being a traitor.

Jesus said something about Judas, which he said about no one else. He did not even comment on the soldiers who beat and killed him. He said that it would have been better that Judas had not been born. Jesus did not say it would have been better that Herod or Pilate had not been born. But he made this comment about his own disciple-turned-traitor. It is clear that Jesus considered disloyal people to be in a different class altogether. You see, an ungrateful traitor is a despicable human being.

Once, I was with a pastor who had been betrayed by his assistant. I talked with him for an hour. He trembled as he spoke about this disloyal minister. He recounted the help he had given to this associate. How he had helped him in school, in marriage and in life. I could almost feel the hatred exuding from this man. At a point, I was even afraid for his health.

If you have not personally experienced disloyalty, you will probably not understand what I am writing about, and I do not blame you. In the world, disloyalty is dealt with ruthlessly and conclusively. Execution is always what to expect.

Hitler's Response to Disloyalty

Hitler, who led Germany into the Second World War, experienced forty-two assassination attempts on his life. During his reign, numerous conspiracies abounded, as is the case with many prominent leaders.

However, Hitler did not fail to respond to the disloyal elements around him. He unleashed an unbridled response to any known conspirators. In one instance, at least five thousand people paid for apparently being disloyal to him!

The landing of the British and the Americans in France and the advance of Soviet troops towards Berlin prompted a group of Germans to conspire, for the last time, against Hitler. Aware that he was leading Germany to utter destruction, they believed that if they continued to accommodate Hitler, the Allies would no longer agree to negotiate with a new post-war German government.

The anti-Hitler conspirators were not well organized, but they managed to recruit Lt.Col. Count Klaus von Stauffenberg, a courageous soldier who had lost an eye, a hand, and two fingers in war for his homeland.

Stauffenberg plotted a coup and undertook to eliminate Hitler personally. When he was invited to a meeting with Hitler at an eastern Prussian outpost, he brought a suitcase containing a time bomb. His intention was to place the suitcase in the bunker where meetings with Hitler were usually held, and then to leave.

The meeting was relocated to a retreat house made of wood, but Stauffenberg continued to seek an opportunity to implement his plan. After Stauffenberg placed the briefcase under the conference-hall table, a short distance from Hitler's legs, he left the room. At 12:37, a loud explosion was heard.

Stauffenberg assumed that Hitler was dead.

He flew to Berlin to join Von Witzleben and Von Beck to take over Germany using the German Home Army. But Hitler was only slightly injured, though three other people were killed. In all about 20 people were wounded in the attack. The reason for the small number of casualties was lucky circumstances, including the fact that somebody moved the briefcase.

Hitler emerged from this attack and was able to keep an appointment with the Italian leader Benito Musolini. He thanked 'fate' for allowing him to continue his 'work' saying, "I am immortal." The next day Hitler made a radio announcement asking every German to redouble their war efforts.

The Fate of the Disloyal Ones

Von Stauffenberg was arrested the same day and shot. The rest of the conspirators were tried and hanged or offered the chance to commit suicide and spare their families.

Eight of those executed were hanged with piano strings from meat-hooks and their executions filmed and shown to senior members of the Nazi Party and the armed forces.

Field Marshal Rommel, wrongly suspected of direct involvement in the conspiracy, was among the suicides; the Germans' official communiqué reported his death as the result of a traffic accident.

In the aftermath, 15,000 people were arrested and 5,000 executed. Several of the most famous conspirators were subjected to abuse and then strangled in an especially slow and brutal manner. By order of Hitler, their executions were filmed and shown to selected audiences as a warning.

Vengeance Is Mine

When ministers experience disloyalty, they often feel like revenging. Like Hitler, they want to lash out at anyone they suspect. But Christian pastors must not behave like Hitler!

We are expected to forgive and love those that hurt us. Many times people do not even know what they are doing to you.

After years of experience with disloyalty, I consider disloyal men to be "painful people" sent to trick you into the sin of unforgiveness. They are agents of the devil sent to pollute your heart with vengeance and wicked ideas. Leave everything in the hands of God!

God is capable of more wickedness than any of us when it comes to vengeance and rewarding of evildoers.

Failing to love will wipe out all your fruits in the ministry.

Ministers will lose their rewards if they do not have love. "If I have the gift of prophecy, and know all mysteries and all knowledge; and if I have all faith, so as to remove mountains, but do not have love, *I am nothing*. All the fruits that should have profited us in heaven will be canceled because we do not have love. And if I give all my possessions to feed the poor, and if I surrender my body to be burned, but do not have love, it profits me nothing" (1Corinthians 13:2-3 NASU).

Why should I allow an accuser to poison me and lead me down the wrong road? That is the real test we face when betrayed. Can you forgive? Can you love? Can you stay the course and continue to do the right thing? Forget about what people think and serve God. No man can reward you. The Lord judges all things. Walk in love. The ultimate trap is to get you out of love.

7. Broken Friendships

For IT WAS NOT AN ENEMY THAT REPROACHED ME; THEN I COULD HAVE BORNE IT: neither was it he that hated me that did magnify himself against me; then I would have hid myself from him: But it was thou, a man mine equal, MY GUIDE, and mine acquaintance. WE TOOK SWEET COUNSEL TOGETHER and walked unto the house of God in company

Psalm 55:12-13

The experience of disloyalty is often heightened by the closeness of the betrayer. King David received much counsel from Ahithophel. As a king could not have many friends, Ahithophel must have been special to David.

It was a great privilege for Ahithophel the Gilonite to be counted as a friend of the king. David lamented about Ahithophel's betrayal and said, "We went to church together"

The rebellion of all the armies of Israel did not mean as much as the betrayal of his friend, Ahithophel.

Six Things That Should Prevent Disloyalty

Psalm 55 reveals David's anguish over Ahithophel's betrayal. This is what he said about Ahithophel.

But it was thou, a man mine equal, my guide, and mine acquaintance. We took sweet counsel together, and walked unto the house of God in company.

Psalm 55:13-14

- A man mine equal... (Being treated as an equal)
- My guide... (Giving guidance)

- Mine acquaintance... (Friendship)
- Mine acquaintance... (knowing someone very well)
- We walked unto the house of God in company... (Going to Church Together)
- We took sweet counsel together... (Discussing issues and enjoying sweet counsel together)

Ideally, this extent of relationship should have prevented anyone from turning against his friend. And yet, Ahithophel, who had these privileges, turned against his friend.

Ahithophel knew that he had done David the maximum evil. That is why he killed himself. Being a wise man, he knew what the end of all traitors was.

He did not want to be around to harvest the fruits of his disloyalty. "Now when Ahithophel saw that his counsel was not followed, he saddled his donkey and arose and went to his home, to his city, and set his house in order, and strangled himself; thus he died and was buried in the grave of his father" (2 Samuel 17:23 NASU)

Powerful Betrayers

The effects of betrayal depend on the rank of the disloyal person. I once knew a minister who had several disloyal associates.

Time and time again pastors would break off and start churches round the corner. Numerous accusations and rumors were bandied about. Somehow, none of these rebellions affected the church until one day the pastor's wife decided to "rebel" against her husband. The effect of his wife's leaving (just as several pastors had left) was much greater. The departure of the wife shook the church to its foundation.

The closer the person the greater the effect of disloyalty!

8. The Pretense

The words of his mouth were smoother than butter, but war was in his heart: his words were softer than oil, yet were they drawn swords.

Psalm 55:21

Ahithophel's words were softer than oil and yet harder and sharper than drawn swords. How could this be? How could the words of his mouth be smoother than butter and war be found in his heart?

Ahithophel was at war with David, but the words of his mouth did not reveal it. There are people who are perfect pretenders. Their ability to flow equally with all sides is a mystery. I find it difficult to pretend and I love to do things, which are real. We all have to accept the reality of bi-polar people - those who operate comfortably at the two poles or extremes.

I Love You and I Don't Love You

One pastor told me about the bi-polar nature of his wife. He told me how she would come to church and be the epitome of pleasantness. He remarked about how she would speak gently and sweetly to everyone.

He recounted, "One day she was making some announcements from the pulpit and said, 'I love my husband and my family so much.' The pastor told me, "I felt like shouting 'You liar. You pretender'.

He told about a terrible experience he had had one night and how he wanted his wife to be near him. "She refused to come to me. I had to get a guard to be with me."

This man was suffering at home from a woman who did not love him anymore. Yet, she was able to outwardly pretend that she enjoyed a sweet and happy marriage. Unfortunately, when these bi-polar people reveal the hidden side it is often unbelievable.

I Am with You and I Am Not with You

There are people who blow both hot and cold air. They produce bitter and sweet waters at the same time. The words of his mouth were smoother than butter. "From the same mouth come both blessing and cursing. My brethren, these things ought not to be this way. Does a fountain send out from the same opening both fresh and bitter water?" (James 3:10-11).

9. Many People Still Love You

He hath delivered my soul in peace from the battle that was against me: FOR THERE WERE MANY WITH ME.

Psalm 55:18

You will also discover that many people truly love their leader and pastor. In spite of attempts to disrupt the ministry, many people remain loyal.

King David had thousands of troops that fought for him. Even though Absalom seemed to have won the hearts of many, many more seemed to still love David. "Then David numbered the people who were with him and set over them commanders of thousands and commanders of hundreds"

(2Samuel 18:1 NASU). So many people were ready to fight for David that he had to appoint commanders of thousands and commanders of hundreds.

Though there are always people who grumble and murmur, you will discover that those that are with you are more than those that are against you. You will succeed if you do not magnify the words and the works of disloyal people. As Elisha said to Gehazi, "... those that are with us are more than those that are against us."

Underdog or Top Dog

I discussed this phenomenon with a friend. The phenomenon of many people staying loyal to the leader in spite of rumors, discontentment, etc.

He simply explained this phenomenon with the statement "People sympathize with the underdog but they follow the top dog…"

10. Pray Hard

As for me, I will call upon God; and the LORD shall save me.

Psalm 55:16 (NASU)

Sadam Hussein was captured not because of the might of the US military. He was captured when someone betrayed him. Betrayal can cause the tide of the battle to turn against you. Dear friend, when you experience wicked and disloyal people it is a signal to pray.

Join David in his prayer, "Evening and morning and at noon, I will complain and murmur, And He will hear my voice. He will redeem my soul in peace from the battle which is against me, For they are many who strive with me. God will hear and answer them -- Even the one who sits enthroned from of old -- Selah. With whom there is no change, And who do not fear God. He has put forth his hands against those who were at peace with him; He has violated his covenant. Cast your burden upon the LORD and He will sustain you; He will never allow the righteous to be shaken" (Psalm 55:17-20).

11. Curses

But You, O God, will bring them down to the pit of destruction; Men of bloodshed and deceit will not live out half their days. But I will trust in You.

Psalm 55:23 (NASU)

It is easy to curse someone like Ahithophel. David cursed Ahithophel, Absalom and all those that betrayed him. A short life was their portion. Do not take the curses of authority figures lightly! An authority figure can be someone like a king, a pastor, a father, a mother or even a teacher. David's curse covered his disloyal son, Absalom.

You Are Cursed without a Pronouncement

Even if the pastor does not curse you, you are cursed when you do things that attract curses. If you break a principle, the principle will break you. Certain actions set eternal forces in motion against you. "The curse of the Lord is in the house of the wicked" (Proverbs 3:33). As you can see, there is an automatic curse on all wicked people.

I Didn't Die, or Did I?

One day, a pastor of a church took over the branch he pastored. He changed the name of the church and set himself up as the sole and final authority of the ministry. It was a sore evil to watch this man illegally possess what was not his. This event also caused much pain to the Body of Christ.

In the intense exchange of words that ensued between the Bishop and his breakaway leader, the Bishop declared, "If you ever stand in the pulpit of my church which you have illegally stolen, you will die on the same day".

This breakaway branch pastor replied, "I shall not die but live."

The next Sunday he went to church and he preached as usual. A week later he bragged, "So and so cursed me and said that if I preached from that pulpit again I would die, but I am still alive. I did not die as he said." He felt he had overcome the curse of his father.

Nevertheless, it is not as simple as that. God warned Adam and Eve that they would die in the day that they ate the fruit. Did they physically die on that day? Certainly not. But death entered their lives on that very day. From that day, they were a living dead couple!

David prayed that his betrayers should not live for even half of their days. "Men of bloodshed and deceit will not live out half their days" (Psalm 55:23 NASU). It is not easy to notice when someone has lived for only half of his days.

Should I Curse My Disloyal Sons?

Should leaders curse their disloyal sons? Should senior pastors curse those who rebel against them? The fact that King David cursed his disloyal friends does not mean we should.

Jesus said something very different, "But I say to you who hear, love your enemies, do good to those who hate you, bless those who curse you, pray for those who mistreat you" (Luke 6:27-28).

Bless them which persecute you: bless, and curse not.

Romans 12:14

One day, I was speaking to a rebellious son. I realized that he was scared that I would curse him.

He blurted out, "Do you want to curse me?"

But I re-assured him and said, "I have not cursed you and I *will not* curse you."

Why should I curse my own son? There are so many problems to deal with without an additional curse. Because of the laws they have broken, disloyal people will have enough trouble anyway. Uncontrollable forces unleashed by sin will fight against the sinner. There is no need for any extra input from me. Moreover, when I make a mistake I would not like anybody to curse me!

Chapter 5

The Scoffers

Blessed is the man that walketh not in the counsel of the ungodly, nor standeth in the way of sinners, nor sitteth in the seat of the scornful.

Psalm 1:1

When I remember the people who have been disloyal to me, all I can think of is men who actually despise me. Disloyal men look down on you and don't think much of what you are and what you can do.

Blessed is the man who does not experience the mocking eyes of disloyal men! Mockers and scoffers will always be a part of the world that we live in. Mockery is a spirit that tries to shut you up and intimidate you. Do not let intimidation stop your ministry.

The Mockers

Sanballat and Tobiah made fun of Nehemiah's attempt to rebuild the wall. They said that if even a fox climbed on the wall they were building it would break it down. "But it came to pass, that when Sanballat heard that we builded the wall, he was wroth, and took great indignation, and mocked the Jews. And he spake before his brethren and the army of Samaria, and said, What do these feeble Jews? will they fortify themselves? will they sacrifice? will they make an end in a day? will they revive the stones out of the heaps of the rubbish which are burned? Now Tobiah the Ammonite was by him, and he said, Even that which they build, if a fox go up, he shall even break down their stone wall" (Nehemiah 4:1-3).

The Spirit of the Scoffer

When somebody has the spirit of a scoffer, he sees all your weaknesses and faults. You do not need disloyal men around you when you begin your ministry. In the beginning of the ministry, you are at the weakest point you will ever be. Your church is at an infantile stage. It is easy to laugh at a six-member church. When there are only twelve people in your church, it is easy for someone to make fun of you.

The spirit of the scoffer tries to stop you in your tracks. It comes to prevent you from going ahead with the vision that God has for you. Through a combination of ridicule and mockery there will be no more spirit left in you to carry on in the ministry. That is why the Scripture blesses the man who does not encounter mockers and scoffers.

You Have Twelve Cells

I remember a pastor who asked about the progress of our ministry. We told him we were doing well and that we then had twelve churches. Then he asked how many people were in each church. We explained that some of them had ten members and others had twenty. Then he laughed and said, "You don't have twelve churches. You have twelve cell groups." I felt so embarrassed when this man of God made fun of our churches.

Be Bold!

Satan keeps you away from boldly engaging in new things through the fear of ridicule.

I remember the first time I baptized somebody. I fumbled with the first person to be baptized and before I realized, my assistant, was laughing at me. I felt so embarrassed and have never forgotten that laugh! But I carried on baptizing and it got better.

Satan knows that feeling and he capitalizes on it anytime there is something bold and new to do. Ridicule is a barrier you must cross. The devil is a bully and he knows your weak areas. Anytime you attempt to go into an area of ministry, he reminds you of your inexperience and lack of power.

When it is time for you to become a pastor, he'll remind you about all your deficiencies and why you do not qualify.

Is He Powerful?

I always remember the first wedding I officiated. The parents of the groom were born-again Christians and they asked who was officiating the wedding. When they found out that it was yours truly, they just asked one question, "Is he powerful?" When I heard that they were asking if I was a powerful minister, I was intimidated and I felt like running away.

He Doesn't Have Miracles

I remember a young man who despised me and left our church. He told everyone, "That guy doesn't have any miracles. There is no power in the church."

I felt embarrassed about it. I felt impotent and useless. The critics continued, "He is just an administrator. He is a white man without power who uses administrative techniques to help the church."

A couple of years later, God blessed me and I began having miracle services. Every time there were miracles, I would remember this person and how he said I didn't have miracles.

You Are Not Always Right!

A brother full of hatred and rebellion said to me, "You are not always right." And he was right. I am not always right! But the spirit with which he told me the truth was that of a scorner. He knew that I was just a man who made mistakes like everyone else. I felt demeaned and I felt like someone was looking down on my humanity.

The reality cannot be denied. I am a human being with frailties and obvious weaknesses. However, to have someone so close to see it all and deride me is a completely different experience. We unconsciously keep away from anything that demeans us. The devil loves to ridicule us. If I had allowed the devil to intimidate me, I would not be in the ministry today.

Silent Mockers

There is also a group of mockers who say little or nothing to you. You must understand that their silence may mean that they despise you and would not even bother to relate or communicate with you. You will notice how uneasy you become in their presence.

Do not allow the devil to intimidate you.

Do not permit anyone into your close circle who despises what you are and what you do.

Get rid of the despising and silent mocking eyes! They are silent but disloyal men. No one can flourish in the midst of these silent scoffers and mockers!

Chapter 6

The Accusers

In your leadership experience, you will meet different kinds of disloyal people. Perhaps one of the most daunting enemies you will ever encounter is 'the accuser in the midst of the brethren'. Problems come in different levels but one of the highest problems is to encounter an accuser in the midst of the brethren.

At the highest point of your ministry, you will struggle with the accuser.

Accusation is Satan's topmost strategy for dealing with an unconquerable enemy. "Now the salvation, and the power, and the kingdom of our God and the authority of His Christ have come, for the accuser of our brethren has been thrown down, he who accuses them before our God day and night" (Revelation 12:10 NASU).

Although the devil is commonly known as the *accuser of the brethren*, he is actually the *accuser in the midst of the brethren*.

Satan's Best Weapon

Satan has different formats by which he operates. He may come to you in the form of a *tempter, a liar, a murderer* or a *deceiver.* However, if he takes you on as an *accuser*, the battle has been lifted to the highest possible level. This principle is played out in the life of Jesus Christ. Initially, the devil came to him in the form of a tempter. Jesus Christ was tempted in the wilderness for forty days. Satan lied to Him in the wilderness and desperately tried to deceive Him.

Throughout his ministry, the Lord was attacked by the devil in the form of a murderer. "He was a murderer from the beginning" (John 8:44). On several occasions Satan tried to kill Jesus through mob action but He would escape. "And they got up and drove Him out of the city, and led Him to the brow of the hill on which their city had been built, in order to throw Him down the cliff. But passing through their midst, He went His way" (Luke 4:29-30 NASU).

On another occasion, the devil tried to drown Jesus in the Sea of Galilee but he was not successful because Jesus rebuked the storm. It was not God who brought the storm; otherwise, Jesus rebuked God's wisdom by rebuking the storm. "But as they sailed he fell asleep: and there came down a storm of wind on the lake; and they were filled with water, and were in jeopardy. And they came to him, and awoke him, saying, Master, master, we perish. Then he arose, and rebuked the wind and the raging of the water: and they ceased, and there was a calm" (Luke 8:23-24 NASU).

Coming in the Garb of an Accuser

However, Jesus' ministry was finally brought to an end when Satan put on the garb of an accuser. Jesus endured one week of intense accusations, which brought His ministry to an end. This week of intensive accusations, started from Palm Sunday until He was crucified. In Matthew 21:1-17, you will see how He entered Jerusalem triumphantly and cleansed the temple. You will notice how the questions and accusations started from the day after He arrived in Jerusalem (Matthew 21:23).

This time Satan pulled out his deadliest weapon and unleashed it against the Lord. The weapon of accusation was finally deployed. For a whole week before the Passover, the Lord was in the temple being questioned and examined (accused) by the Pharisees. "Then went the Pharisees, and took counsel how they might ENTANGLE HIM in his talk. And they sent out unto him their disciples with the Herodians, saying, Master, we know that thou art true, and teachest the way of God in truth, neither carest thou for any man: for thou regardest not the person of men. Tell us therefore, What thinkest thou? Is it lawful to give tribute unto Caesar, or not? But Jesus perceived their WICKEDNESS, and said, Why TEMPT ye me, ye hypocrites?"(Matthew 22:15-18).

The Lord was questioned about every aspect of His life and ministry. For several days, the Lord endured the wickedness and hypocrisy of those who questioned him in the temple. In the last twenty-four hours of His life, He was also accused in the palace of the high priest, in Pilate's court and also in Herod's palace.

Jesus met this series of high-level accusations with a variety of responses. He answered the temple questions succinctly and made fools out of His accusers. "When they had heard these words, they marveled, and left him, and went their way" (Matthew 22:22). They had never heard anything like that before. "The officers answered, Never man spake like this man" (John 7:46). However, when in the court of Pilate and other heathen rulers, he answered nothing to the questions that were leveled at Him. "And he answered him to never a word; insomuch that the governor marvelled greatly" (Matthew 27:14).

As you can see, Satan has different guises under which he attacks. Perhaps you suffer from a plague of accusations in the ministry. Often you do not understand what is happening to you.

What Is an Accusation?

An accusation is a charge or allegation made against someone. It puts blame and points fingers at a person. An accusation is a statement saying that you think someone is guilty of doing something wrong, especially of committing a crime. These statements, which are directed at a person, constantly minister *a withering and weakening guilt.* Only very strong-hearted people can live with persistent accusations for a long time.

Even though accusations come out of human mouths, they are anointed by the accuser of the brethren himself. Satan is the accuser in the midst of the brethren.

Disloyal Men Are Commonly Employed As Accusers

In my country, some people are commonly employed as security guards. There are also people who are commonly employed as butchers and *khebab* sellers. Similarly, there are some people whom Satan commonly employs as accusers. Simply put, accusers are basically disloyal men.

They also fall into the category I call 'familiar friends' of the accused. "Yea, mine own familiar friend, in whom I trusted, which did eat of my bread, hath lifted up his heel against me" (Psalm 41:9).

Familiar friends who become disloyal are very dangerous. They are the familiar people of your life who have turned against you; that is friends, husbands, wives, sons, daughters, beloveds, associate pastors, church members, journalists, classmates and the like. For accusations to have any impact, they must be channeled through someone close.

Why Not Simply Brush off Accusations?

Are accusations not statements that are true or false? If they are not true, why don't you just ignore them? But it is never as easy as that.

Accusations are anointed from Hell.

Accusations are spiritual things.

Accusations are tiny arrows loaded with satanic poison.

As soon as the poison enters your blood, it spreads through your whole being attacking your heart. Like some fast-spreading natural poison, you are greatly affected by a seemingly little dart. I have seen mighty giants of God totally ruffled by unfounded accusations which looked insignificant to the bystander. Such is the power of accusation. It is a puzzling weapon and its effects are mysterious. Truly, accusations are spiritual weapons.

The Pointing of the Finger

> Then **YOUR LIGHT WILL BREAK OUT LIKE THE DAWN,** And your recovery will speedily spring forth; And your righteousness will go before you; The glory of the LORD will be your rear guard. Then you will call, and the LORD will answer; You will cry, and He will say, "Here I am.' IF YOU REMOVE the yoke from your midst, **THE POINTING OF THE FINGER** and speaking wickedness...
>
> **Isaiah 58:8-9 (NASU)**

Accusations are also called "the pointing of the finger". Such is the evil released by the pointing of the finger, that the light in your life and ministry will actually grow dim from it.

Your light will break forth like the dawn and there will be recovery if you put away the pointing of the finger!

Ministries cannot prosper once a disloyal finger-pointing person is allowed to flourish nearby. Much of the darkness in the Body of Christ is as a result of the incessant accusations made by brother against brother, sister against sister, husband against wife, and so on. You must know the people around you who are used to accuse you.

Every good leader must understand the principles of accusation. You can wither and weaken in ministry through diverse accusations! Your ministry can actually be misdirected by accusations. I have experienced that myself.

The book of Revelation shows how God dealt decisively with the Accuser of the Brethren. It reveals four amazing benefits of silencing accusations. In these four benefits, we see everything that we desire from God: strength, salvation, power and the Kingdom of God. O how much power and strength will be released into your life if the pointing of the finger was not there!

Most ordinary people do not feel that they are qualified to serve God. Most of the people I have trained in the ministry were discouraged and accused by the devil. But I simply encouraged them constantly to serve God and become priests in spite of their shortcomings.

This encouragement was completely contrary to the voice of the accuser in their lives. That voice told them they were not good enough! But my constant encouragement to serve God and to trust Him silenced the voice of the accuser. Suddenly, weak and incapable people received salvation, power and strength to do God's work.

Deal with Disloyal Accusers

And I heard a loud voice saying in heaven, Now is come SALVATION, and STRENGTH, and the KINGDOM OF OUR GOD, and the POWER OF HIS CHRIST: for the accuser of our brethren is cast down, which ACCUSED them before our God day and night.

Revelation 12:10

This Scripture shows four clear blessings of dealing with accusers.

Salvation is the first benefit of silencing accusers in your midst.

Strength is the next important benefit for eliminating accusers from your little fellowship.

The Kingdom of our God will come when the accuser of the brethren is cast down.

Finally, the power of Christ is released when the accuser is dealt with.

All these benefits are clearly outlined in the Scripture as being things that happen when the accuser is silenced. If you allow an associate minister to point fingers at you, you will be weakened and the power of God in your life will be reduced. The salvation and the coming of God's kingdom are dependent on your dealing with the accuser.

Chapter 7

Forgetful Men

Amongst the men you will work with are men who do not have the ability to remember. Ungrateful men are a most deadly group. They are the brewing conspirators of your ministry. They are the up and coming traitors of your team.

The ability to remember is probably the single most important quality for a minister. If I discover that, I am walking with someone who has the ability to remember I relax. Almost every disloyal person lacks the ability to remember! When I think of some of the dangerous sons that I have had I wonder if they cannot remember the times I had with them.

When the children of Israel were coming out of Egypt, remembrance was one thing God wanted them to have. He wanted them to remember how he had brought them out of Egypt. He wanted them to remember how bad things had been. In their prosperity, He wanted them to be grateful to the Lord God. God knew what would happen if they forgot these important things. When you do not remember you become disloyal and unfaithful to the calling and commission of God. Many ministers have become unfaithful to the mission of Christ because they have forgotten too many things.

In the next section, I want to share about why it is important to remember. Remembrance is the master key to loyalty. Failing to remember creates disloyalty!

Why it Is Important to Remember

1. Remembering makes you grateful.

Ungrateful men sing songs that show their short memory. Most Christians are not grateful to God for their salvation.

Sadly, many Christians do not remember what Christ has done for them. The songs composed and sang by Christians today reflect this forgetful and unfaithful attitude. My heart jumps when I hear songs about salvation. Perhaps, this is why I love songs that speak of our salvation.

Ungrateful men do not evangelize. They have forgotten how salvation came to them. They have even forgotten how salvation gets to anyone. Pastors who have forgotten about their salvation preach without doing altar calls. Ungrateful men have substituted the message of salvation for the popular motivational sermons on finance, management and "prosperity". These messages may be good but they cannot be *substituted* for the message of salvation.

It is forgetful men who go round the world giving out food and water to sinners without ever preaching to them. Perhaps they have forgotten that no one will go to Heaven unless he is born again. Churches are filled with happy-go-lucky Christians who want to celebrate their prosperity without a thought about how they were saved. What about others? Would I have been saved if no one had remembered?

2. Remembering makes you accommodate others.

Remembrance is important because it is supposed to govern your current behavior. "And thou shalt remember that thou wast a bondman in Egypt: and thou shalt observe and do these statutes" (Deut 16:12). The Israelites were supposed to remember their past and allow this memory to influence their current behavior.

In the Scripture I just quoted, remembering their past state of being bondmen would propel them to obey the Lord and include fatherless, widows and strangers in their feasts of rejoicing. "And thou shalt rejoice before the LORD thy God, thou, and thy son, and thy daughter, and thy manservant, and thy maidservant, and the Levite that is within thy gates, and the stranger, and the fatherless, and the widow, that are among you, in the place which the LORD thy God hath chosen to place his name there. And thou shalt remember that thou wast a bondman in Egypt: and thou shalt observe and do these statutes." (Deuteronomy 16:11-12)

You Can't Stay Here

When you do not remember where you came from, you behave wrongly. One day, I noticed a lady who was constantly irritated by a stream of cousins, nieces and nephews who were living with her. She did not want to have all these relations living in her house. She wanted her privacy. She wanted to enjoy her husband, her home and her children without interruption. But her husband insisted on having all these cousins, nieces, nephews and miscellaneous relations in the house. It was because of the conflict this situation was bringing that I became aware of the problem.

One day I asked my wife, "What type of home did this lady grow up in? Did she live with her Daddy, her Mummy and other brothers and sisters?" (You see my wife knows everything).

My wife smiled and answered, "No, not at all, she didn't."

"So what kind of home did she grow up in?" I asked.

"Oh, she lived with her aunty for most of her early days. Her mother was far away for most of her childhood and she grew up living in other people's homes."

Then I thought to myself, "Has this lady forgotten that she was a guest and maybe a bother to someone for many years? Can she not accommodate relatives as she was once accommodated?" The problem is that people forget where they came from.

3. Remembering makes you help others.

I remember that it was not easy to break out in ministry. I felt so intimidated by senior "big shot" ministers. They commanded crowds and crowds of people and seemed so powerful. How would my ministry ever be like this? I wondered.

Are You Mocking Me?

One afternoon, I met the pastor of a large church at a social function. He looked me up and down and said, "*Pastor* Dag." When he addressed me as "Pastor", I felt as though the rain of mockery was showering down on me. I withered under his

Forgetful Men

mocking smile. You see, I had about twenty people in my church and he had thousands! I felt like an idiot. His voice reeked of contempt. I almost blurted out, "Are you mocking me?" I felt no help from this great man of God - only mockery.

When I began my church, I made several efforts to be accepted and to gain help. I went to see the pastor of a large church in my city. I had to travel to the upscale part of the city to see this pastor. He graciously received me and sat with me in his garden. I told him how I had begun a church. When he began to talk, however, I wished I had never gone there.

Go to Bible School

He said, "There are many young boys who are starting churches without attending Bible schools. They do not know what they are doing. They will all amount to nothing." Every time I read the comment that Nabal made about David, I remember that day because the remarks Nabal made about David were very similar to what this man of God said to me.

And Nabal answered David's servants, and said, Who is David? and who is the son of Jesse? there be many servants now a days that break away every man from his master.

1 Samuel 25:10

Instead of helping me, he sent his associate pastor to organize a large crusade right where I had started the church. During the programme, they showed a documentary of this pastor's ministry and I felt foolish for even trying to begin a church.

I did not give up. I was still looking for recognition and help for my fledgling church. I invited another well-known pastor to minister in my baby church. This fellow had ministered in my fellowship many times.

Who Are the Thorns?

This time he told my assistant who was sent to invite him that he would not come. "Why not," I asked. My pastor was hesitant to answer my question.

Finally, he did. The "big minister" had said "I have stopped sowing amongst thorns."

"Thorns?" I asked. "Who are the thorns? When did we become thorns? He doesn't want to preach to us anymore?" I questioned.

"Yes," the messenger answered. "He will not come to this new church and he has given the reason. He does not sow among thorns anymore."

Nobody helped us when we were small. And I remember each encounter. That is why I try to help others in ministry. I love to encourage up and coming ministers and to tell them that they are going to make it. Nobody ever told me that. Even up till now, nobody tells me that I am going to make it. It is a great thing to have encouragement.

4. **Remembering makes you walk in your calling**

> And **THOU SHALT REMEMBER that thou wast a bondman in the land of Egypt, and the LORD thy God redeemed thee: therefore I command thee this thing to day.**
>
> **Deuteronomy 15:15**

The Memory of Salvation in School

I remember that I got saved in secondary school. I was about fifteen years old when I found the Lord. The memory of how I found Christ stays with me. I feel so blessed and favored to be chosen and saved. The memory of it guides me in my current ministry. I find myself preaching in schools and universities. I have great hope when I see young boys and girls walking forward to receive Jesus Christ. I remember that I too gave my heart to the Lord in school. Some people seem to remember nothing. Perhaps salvation means nothing to them.

Some men who were raised in orphanages remember how they were shown the love of God. Some of them have built orphanages and cared for other children because they remember everything. Others walk away and rewrite their history by deleting every memory of the orphanage.

The Memory of the Missionaries

The memory of what God has brought you through is supposed to guide your present day ministry. When I see the cemeteries of white missionaries, I remember how they shed their blood on Ghanaian soil for the salvation of an entire nation. Then I think of other remote nations which are waiting for similar missionaries to come. "Will anyone go?" I ask myself. "Will an entire nation perish because there is no missionary?" I remember the sacrifice of these Swiss missionaries with gratitude. It is because Ghanaian churches are led by pastors who have *forgotten* about how missionaries came to die in Ghana, that they do not send missionaries to other similarly deprived areas.

5. Remembering makes you kind.

God told the Israelites to be kind to strangers just because *they* were once foreigners in Egypt. "You shall not oppress a stranger, since you yourselves know the feelings of a stranger, for you also were strangers in the land of Egypt" (Exodus 23:9 NASU).

I remember how I suffered under the repression of some lecturers in medical school. Many lecturers only had threats and warnings for their students. I thought to myself, "If I was ever a lecturer I would be kind to the students and help them to pass their exams."

One day however, I was chatting with one of my classmates and he said, "When I become a lecturer I will ensure that students suffer as much as I did." I was amazed at this declaration. Could he not see what he was going through? Would he not remember the anguish that we experienced in this place? Unfortunately, many wicked people simply cannot remember what it was like to be on the other side.

God warns us in His word to remember how we felt and to help others who are in a similar situation. Perhaps you come from a very poor background. God expects you to reach out and help such poor people because you know what it feels like to be poor!

6. Remembering keeps you humble.

When you remember where you came from, you always recognize that the grace of God has been at work. When you clearly remember where God picked you up from, you will not attribute your current success to any personal strengths or wisdom. Unfortunately, people tend to black out their past. They refer to no one and they seem to remember nothing bad or difficult from their background.

Listening to them, you get the impression that they are self-made. They do not mention their beginnings, their struggles or their failings. You almost get the impression that you are reading about superman when you read about them!

But Paul said that he took pleasure in his infirmities and distressing situations. Paul told us that he had been beaten, and whipped by unbelievers. This does not sound like superman.

Talking plainly about things God has brought you through will only make you thankful and humble. It will save you from self deception and unnecessary pride. "Most gladly, therefore, I will rather boast about my weaknesses, so that the power of Christ may dwell in me" (2 Corinthians 12:9).

A man of remembrance stays humble through the memories of his different trials and sufferings. It is wiser to share these difficulties than to share your victories. I have noticed how the Lord has helped me to share my uselessness with others. Sometimes I end my sermons on a note of weakness and defeat. I take pleasure in the weakness that is real so that the power of Christ will rest on me.

I have seen the dead raised in my ministry but I have also seen many people die after I prayed for them. There are times I share the powerlessness and uselessness of my life and ministry. I am learning to choose this way so that the power of Christ will rest on me. There is no need to protect an image which needs no protection. Be real! Remember the realities of your life. Share them and help yourself to be humble.

7. Remembering makes you a grateful person.

The sin of ungratefulness is as the sin of forgetfulness. They are almost synonymous. Sadly, people forget how they have been loved. Because people forget exactly how they were helped, they are indifferent to the source of help. Some parents virtually have to beg their children to remember them in their old age. Some pastors virtually have to beg their congregations to honor them for their labors.

This world has six billion ungrateful and forgetful people! This is what creates the discontentment, conflict and wars. There are people we must be grateful to. God wants us to be thankful and grateful for all His blessings. We must be grateful for the channels that God uses. We must be grateful for their faithfulness with what God gave to them.